TRUSTING THE ROAD

TRUSTING THE ROAD

One Woman's Walk Around the World for Peace and the Environment

The Story of Teru Imai

By Soren Gordhamer

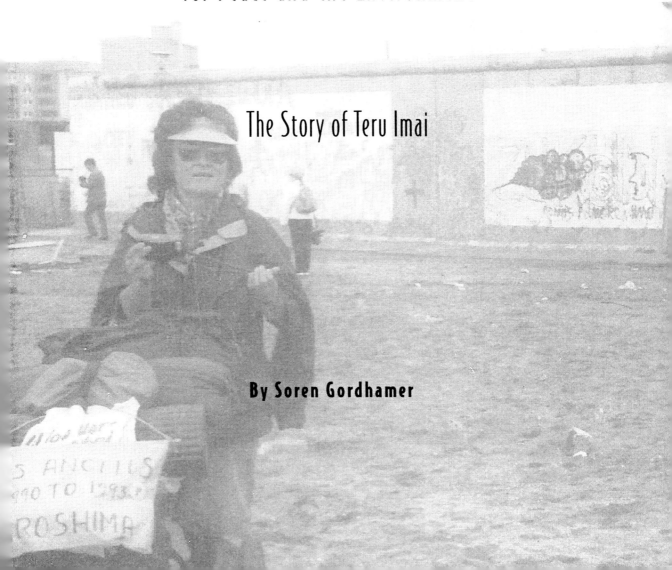

© 2010 Soren Gordhamer
PO Box 562
Dixon, NM 87527
505-692-0240
www.trustingtheroad.com

Cover photograph by Abigail Bokaer.
Back cover portrait by Catherine Ames.
Interior photographs by Catherine Ames, Abigail Bokaer, Essrea Cherin, Greg Edblom, and Soren Gordhamer.
Graphic design by Maile McGrew-Fredé.

This edition printed on demand by Lulu.com.

Library of Congress Cataloguing in Publication
    Trusting the road: one woman's walk around the world for peace
and the environment / by Soren Gordhamer.

ISBN 978-57805398-1
    1.Activists   2. Asian American women   3. Social movements-- 20th century 4. Hiroshima-shi (Japan)
I. Gordhamer, Soren

For Teru

in grateful thanks

"In the beginning, it sounded so noble to walk across the world for peace and the environment. I wanted to be a part of the solution, not a part of the problem. However, in the end the 'doing good' wasn't the main event. The main event was what I learned about myself."

— **Teru Imai**

Photo List

1. *Teru at the Berlin Wall*, by Catherine Ames — i

2. *On the Road Portrait*, by Catherine Ames — iv

3. *Cross Country*, Europe, by Catherine Ames — x

4. *The Walk Begins*, Santa Monica, CA, (From the collection of Abigail Bokaer) — 4

5. *Camping in Nevada* (From the collection of Abigail Bokaer) — 9

6. *End of US Walk*, NYC, (From the collection of Greg Edblom) — 26

7. *Rusting Spoons at Auschwitz*, by Catherine Ames — 34

8. *Cobbled Road I*, Eastern Europe, by Catherine Ames — 48

9. *Taz and Star*, by Soren Gordhamer — 53

10. *Budapest Walkers*, (Taz, Carolyn, Teru, Essrea, Star, Abigail; collection of Abigail Bokaer) — 56

11. *Other Travelers*, Eastern Europe, by Catherine Ames — 59

12. *Breakfast Table*, Eastern Europe, by Catherine Ames (Left to right: Carolyn, Birgitt, Teru) — 61

13. *Resting*, Eastern Europe (Left to right: Birgitt, Carolyn, Teru) — 65

14. *Cobbled Road II*, Eastern Europe, by Catherine Ames — 68

15. *Train Coming*, Eastern Europe, by Catherine Ames — 74

16. *Taj Mahal* (Samazuchi Shoni, Essrea, Teru, Abigail, Mohammad Usman) — 76

17. *Walkers w/ Sunil Dutt in India* — 82

18. *Delhi, India* (From the collection of Abigail Bokaer) — 90

19. *With children in Pakistan*, by Soren Gordhamer — 98

20. *Group Shot*, Northern Pakistan (From the collection of Essrea Cherin) — 111

21. *Step by Step*, Kashgar, China by Soren Gordhamer — 114

22. *Essrea and Teru in Thailand* (From the collection of Essrea Cherin) — 122

23. *Walking in Pakistan* (Star, Teru and Essrea; collection of Essrea Cherin) — 127

24. *In Southeast Asia* (Teru, Hillby, Taz, Abigail, Essrea; collection of Abigail Bokaer) — 132

25. *Prayer Circle*, Hokkaido Japan (From the collection of Essrea Cherin) — 138

26. *Walking with the monks*, Hokkaido Japan (From the collection of Abigail Bokaer) — 143

27. *Peace Flame*, Peace Park, Hiroshima, Japan (From the collection of Abigail Bokaer) — 148

28. *The Journey Ends*, Hiroshima, Japan (From the collection of Abigail Bokaer) — 150

29. *Group shot*, Hiroshima Japan (From the collection of Abigail Bokaer) — 151

30. *Teru visiting with Soren*, Big Sur, California (collection of Soren Gordhamer) — 154

31. *End of Walk Circle*, Hiroshima (From the collection of Abigail Bokaer) — 156

Contents

Introduction 1

1. Santa Monica, California: First Steps 5

2. Lessons from Walking in the U.S. .15

3. New York City 27

4. Lessons from Walking in England, Holland, Poland, and Germany 35

5. Budapest, Hungary 49

6. Lessons from Walking in Hungary, Bulgaria, and Yugoslavia 57

7. Athens, Greece 69

8. Lessons from Walking in India 77

9. Delhi, India 91

10. Lessons from Walking in Pakistan 99

11. Kashgar, China 115

12. Lessons from Walking in Nepal, Thailand, and Cambodia 123

13. Phnom Penh, Cambodia 133

14. Lessons from Walking in Vietnam and Japan 139

15. Peace Park, Hiroshima, Japan .149

16. The Final Years 155

Other Reflections 159

Introduction: The Vision

Many of us who knew and walked with Teru Imai often wondered how we might share more of her life and her story. I had started to help Teru write a book on the three and a half years she spent walking across the globe. Sadly, she died of cancer before we could finish it. One of her fellow-walkers, Larry (Taz) Abele, had the idea of taking her writing and adding to it our own stories and reflections. This is the result of that effort.

Though the Walk in the U.S. regularly had between fifty and a hundred members, in Europe and Asia it was usually just a handful. Taz was with her in the U.S. and for segments in Eastern Europe and Asia, while I participated in the U.S., Pakistan, and Japan. Two other U.S. walkers, Abigail Bokaer and Essrea Cherin, met up with Teru in Budapest, Hungary, and accompanied her for much of the next two years. Since we were all in our early to mid-twenties and Teru was in her early fifties, she was not only the heart and soul of the journey but a mentor and a guide to us all.

It is not easy to explain why a fifty-year-old woman would spend years walking for peace. While most of her friends were sleeping in comfortable beds and living in temperature-controlled homes, Teru was walking along the open road, usually not knowing where she would sleep on any given night or where her next meal would appear. Many people have asked how she initially decided to embark on such a journey, particularly at her age. It is often hard enough to decide to switch jobs or to move from one city to another—how do you decide to leave your job, your work, and your home to undertake a three-and-a-half-year walk across the earth?

The opportunity that was presented to Teru in 1989, called the Global Walk for a Livable World, was the vision of a friend of hers, a lecturer and teacher in Ithaca, New York, named Joan Bokaer. After participating for several weeks in the

Great Peace March, an anti-nuclear-weapons walk across the U.S. in 1986, Joan decided that the time was ripe for a walk in support of the environment and a more "livable world." For Teru, it came at just the right time. The decision to join, she said, was not based on rational thinking. As soon as she heard of the journey, something inside her said, "Yes. This is for you."

This is the story of Teru's experiences on the journey, which she began in February of 1990 and completed in August of 1993. (She was the only member of the group to be on the voyage for its entirety.) In her three and a half years walking, Teru was challenged in ways she never imagined. During the Walk, her will was consistently put to the test—through snow in Greece, torrential monsoons in India, poverty and land mines in Cambodia, and blistering summer heat in Japan. Accompanied by a small group of usually three to five people in Europe and Asia, with no support vehicles, no computer, no cell phone, often no map, and usually no understanding of the local language, she walked almost every day.

As if this were not enough, Teru also carried the Hiroshima Peace Flame for

much of the journey. The flame, which is housed at Peace Park in Hiroshima, was placed in the park after the bombing there in 1945, and Japan has promised to keep it lit until the world is rid of nuclear weapons. Teru sought to carry the flame across the world and return it to its home in Peace Park, the final destination of the Walk. To travel with the flame, she converted a baby jogger to carry the lantern, fuel, and other supplies that she needed. This allowed her to keep the flame in the lantern at night and transport it during the day by lighting small pieces of charcoal in a metal case, or handwarmer.

This book is not a detailed travelogue of her journey. For one, Teru did not keep much of a journal; more important, though, the specifics of her trek did not matter to her. When she started to outline this book, it was not important to her how many steps she took or how many countries she traversed; what mattered were the lessons that she had learned along the way. She knew that very few people would decide to embark on a similar journey. The point of writing a book was not to convince other people to walk long distances; it was to share the wisdom she had gathered from her voyage, which she believed had relevance to all people. This book attempts to share some of those lessons.

There is, of course, no way to fully describe in writing the spirit of a person, but it is my hope that this book will give a snapshot of the courage and wisdom of Teru. You may find, as many of us who knew her did, that her approach to life provides an extraordinary model of what is possible. While the book focuses primarily on Teru's life, specifically her years walking, in a very real way it is also a story about all of us—all of us who seek to follow our vision and make a difference in the world; all of us who want to align our deepest aspirations with our actions; all of us who strive to test our limits.

The book shifts between the stages of Teru's journey, indicated by geographic location, and the lessons that she learned along the way. I have tried to include each lesson in the section of her journey where she discovered it and applied it most frequently, though some lessons do not fit easily in any one section. The material that follows was derived from the beginnings of the book that she started before she died, memories of those who walked with her, and letters she wrote. This book is a tribute to Teru from those of us who knew her and walked with her. It is our testament that one person really can, and in fact did, make a difference.

Santa Monica, California: First Steps

Long before Al Gore considered making a documentary on climate change or Google decided to "go green" and erect the world's largest corporate solar installation at its world headquarters, several hundred people gathered in Santa Monica, California, on February 1, 1990, to take action. Their form of speaking out: a three-and-a-half-year Global Walk in support of the environment. This was the vision, but few knew at the time if the journey would continue after the U.S. segment, or even if they would be able to successfully make it across the U.S. The roughly 125 people who showed up for the initial phase across the U.S. ranged in age from fourteen months to seventy-two years, and included lawyers, college students, hippies, and teachers.

The participants were filled with excitement on this sunny winter day, ready to begin the 3,000-mile trek across the U.S., which was scheduled to end in New York City on United Nations Day, October 24th. The organizers of the Walk hoped that the initial nine month journey through 350 cities would serve as a wake-up call to help forge a more sustainable path that addressed issues such as climate change, species loss, and ozone depletion. In an attempt to live what they preached along the way, the group would keep a vegetarian diet and sleep in tents out in fields or indoors in churches and community centers

As the group huddled near the beach, an array of support vehicles waited nearby; these would keep the hundred or so walkers fed and sheltered as they traversed fifteen to twenty miles a day. Three were converted school buses: one had ten low-flush toilets, and was called, appropriately, "the potty bus"; another was adapted to carry tents, backpacks, and other luggage from one destination to the next; and a third was renovated as a communications bus, with computers and a space bridge antenna for communicating via satellite. There was also a shiny white refrigerator truck, with a wind generator attached to the roof; a kitchen trailer powered by solar panels and equipped with a stove, an oven, and other cooking necessities; two trailers with 500-gallon water tanks; and a purple Toyota van known affectionately as the "blister bus," which would follow walkers and pick up the tired, the sick, and the injured.

For most people, joining the journey was not easy. They had to take time off from or quit their jobs, raise the $3,000 fee to help cover costs, and live primarily without generating income for this period. But people found a way. One woman, Gabriella Cower, a language specialist from Spain, heard about the Walk only three weeks before the start date. She quickly rented her apartment, sold her car, wrote up a will, and bought a ticket to Los Angeles to be with the group on February 1st. Others left college on a moment's notice or decided that instead of attending Lion's Club meetings and going on fishing trips in their retirement they would walk across the country. Joining took a particular courage, since at this time there was much less awareness about the severity of the global environmental situation. Many parents did not understand why their children would leave college to join the Global Walk, apparently showing more concern about the planet than a career. And grown children were often flabbergasted that their mothers and grandmothers would choose to leave a comfortable home with air-conditioning, heating, and cable television to live for nine months in a tent, all for what they viewed as a hard-to-define cause.

Still, people from various backgrounds found their way to the group. They included a tall, lanky Florida native named Larry (Taz) Abele, in his early twenties, who had taken the bus down from Oregon, where he had been building houses with Habitat for Humanity. He had heard of the Global Walk while watching a video of an earlier walk, focused on anti-nuclear issues, called the Great Peace March. He was instantly hooked. There was Essrea Cherin, also in her twenties, who was living and working at a community in Arizona when she heard of it; and Ilyse Simon, an enthusiastic student from Brandeis University, in Massachusetts, who knew when she heard about the Walk that it was for her. Abigail Bokaer, a buoyant, brown-haired young woman from Ithaca, New York, had also left college to join. Her mother, Joan, the Walk's visionary, encouraged her by saying, "College will always be there, but this Walk will not."

A sprightly blond twenty-year-old college student named Inga Star Van Kreidt (who went by "Star") arrived from Chico, California, after hearing about the journey from a member of the Great Peace March. There was a hotel inspector from Minnesota named Aledia Van Dyke, who, at seventy-two years of age, was the elder of the group. Among the international participants were a Japanese Buddhist monk from Tokyo named Immamura and a secondary-school teacher from Minsk named Svetlana Tiernchenko, who was accompanied by her ten-year-old daughter, Katya.

Standing with them by the ocean in front of the Sea Castle Apartments in Santa Monica, listening to music and eating free ice cream provided by Ben and Jerry's, was a fifty-year-old Japanese-American, Teru Imai. The five-foot-four former dental hygienist, who had one grown son, had spent that morning making last-minute decisions about what to bring on the journey. Did she need a camera? Yes, she answered herself, I need to document this with pictures. How about an umbrella? No, she surmised, I'll just bring a rain poncho. How about an outdoor camp chair for sitting? No, I can sit on the ground. After reviewing her list and checking it several times, she included in her backpack, along with these items, a pair of Teva sandals, green and brown hiking boots, a journal, several changes of clothes, toiletries, and lantern fuel and other necessities to keep the Peace Flame lit.

A few months earlier, Teru had quit her job as a teacher/administrator at Allied Health College, in North Hollywood, and leased her condo to help finance the trip. In her words, "I was at the point in my life when I felt like stretching myself and reaching farther." Now, standing with the others, Teru enjoyed the festivities around her: a group of walkers played music in the distance, several Japanese monks beat drums while chanting for peace, schoolchildren dipped their hands in paint and placed them on a mural to help decorate it, a Native American elder held a ceremony on the beach, and several people held flags—one of the U.S., one of the United Nations, and one showing the earth from space—high in the air. After a year of planning, the group was starting to come alive. The Walk that Teru had been waiting for was getting ready to take its first steps.

Teru recognized a number of the walkers from meetings she had attended in the Los Angeles area. Those who were unknown to her, she figured, she would soon get a chance to know much better from months together on the road. Teru noticed the new shoes and clean shirts that many people wore, and she guessed that they would not stay that way long from the wear and tear of "walk life." Teru sensed that she, too— like people's clothes—would change in ways that she could not foresee. The weather, the people, the walking . . . all would have an impact on her. In joining the trek, she knew that her life would never be the same.

As the group assembled, Teru remembered why the Walk was important to her.

She recalled the struggle she had felt as a four-year-old girl trying to understand why the two countries that she knew best—the U.S., where she had been born, and Japan, where her ancestors lived—had gone to war. And why her own country had placed her in an internment camp during the war. "If I am American," she wondered at the time, "why would my own country imprison me just because of my ancestry?" Her confusion was exacerbated by the fact that she had relatives in Pearl Harbor, matriarchal roots in Hiroshima, and an uncle fighting in the 442nd U.S. Army Battalion in Italy at the time she was in the camp.

She did not understand this as a young girl, and still did not as she was about to take her first steps as a member of the Global Walk for a Livable World. What she did know was that war had scarred many people, both visibly and invisibly, and that it was the responsibility of every person to be an exemplary citizen in, and work for, a livable world. What this meant exactly she did not know, but the Walk was the best way she knew to express her concern and commitment.

Standing with the group, she recalled the concerns expressed by friends and family who could not understand why she was undertaking such a journey. Some wondered about her safety. "Couldn't you easily be hit by a car walking alongside highways?" they asked. Others doubted her physical strength: "You are fifty years old—do you really think you  can walk 3,000 miles across the country?" Still others wondered how she would adapt to the lifestyle: "You mean, you just walk every day? What will you do for entertainment? You are going to live without television and a phone for months.

Are you crazy?" Teru had little concern for her safety or her ability to entertain herself on the journey, but she did wonder if her half-century-old legs could make it. She had never been very athletic or much of a hiker. Her preparation—walking ten miles every weekend during the previous few months—was nothing like regularly trekking fifteen to twenty miles a day for several months.

Though she had some doubts about her physical ability, Teru knew, standing with the others, that she had made the right decision. This was exactly where she belonged. In fact, her entire life had led up to this point. Her internment as a child, her years working for racial equality, her joining the Asian-Americans for Peace to support nuclear disarmament—all of these were preparations for the Walk.

As she reflected on the activities that led to this day, a voice boomed over a loudspeaker, "Walkers, let's go. The Global Walk for a Livable World has officially begun." This was met by cheers, applause, and a slow movement forward. Teru took her first step, having no idea at the time that during the next three and a half years she would walk about nine thousand miles through more than twenty countries. She had no way of knowing then how much joy, laughter, and discovery lay ahead, or the amount of struggle and pain. But, once she took that first step, her body filled with energy, and it became instantly clear that she was going to walk just as far as her legs and determination would allow her.

Teru was not alone in her desire to use this three-million-year-old method—still the most common form of transportation in the world—to initiate both internal and external change. From a historical perspective, Teru might not have been as crazy as she seemed. The Australian Aborigines used "walkabouts," which usually lasted from six months to a year, as a rite of passage for young people in their early teens. The Basques in France reportedly did something similar. Numerous North American indigenous tribes valued walking and traveling as a way to gain vision and to better connect to the great spirit of life.

In fact, walking with a purpose has been found useful by more than just youth in indigenous cultures. Writers and philosophers for generations have relied on walking for inspiration and clarity. Throughout his life, Soren Kierkegaard took daily walks in his beloved Copenhagen to help focus his thinking, to get fresh air, and to observe people. He did this so often that one of his nieces is reported to have called the streets Kierkegaard's "reception room." Jean-Jacques Rousseau, the Swiss-born philosopher, used walking in much the same way. William Wordsworth, at twenty-one, set off on a two-thousand-mile journey on foot, and years later took shorter walks as he developed his poetry. In college, while he was supposed to be studying for exams, he and a friend ventured off by foot across France and into the Alps. Thoreau valued walking to such a degree that he wrote one of his most famous articles on the subject. The environmentalist John Muir was first inspired to actively protect wild lands after his walk from Indiana to the Florida Keys, recalled in his memoir of that journey, A Thousand-Mile Walk to the Gulf. Years later, he would spend months walking in the woods, getting to know intimately the trees and mountains of the Sierras and using that knowledge in his environmental advocacy.

The spiritual seeker has also set out on pilgrimages, usually by foot, to find a teacher or to deepen understanding. Buddha, Jesus, and Muhammad all traveled primarily by foot. Social activists, too, have seen the power of walking as a means of advocating change and expressing disagreement with government policies. At the March on Washington for Jobs and Freedom, in 1963, Martin Luther King, Jr., and more than a quarter million others of many races loudly and effectively demanded equal rights. When the British in India imposed a new tax on salt in 1930, Mohandas K. Gandhi and others took to their feet to express disapproval, trekking 250 miles to the sea in protest. Their legendary walk, known as the Salt March, became one of the most successful actions during India's quest for independence.

No single reason has drawn people to venture long distances by foot. One man, Steve Vaught, reportedly walked across the United States to lose weight. He started the website www.thefatmanwalking.com to document the journey. While visiting my father in Texas in the mid-nineties, I read a story in the local paper about a man walking through the town on a cross-country trek. I guessed his route, located him on a highway just outside town, and invited him back home for dinner and an overnight stay. Over a spaghetti dinner, he claimed to be walking just for fun. He carried a duffel bag full of magazines and romance novels, and was unlike any other walker I had previously met.

Probably the most well-known peace walker in the U.S. was Peace Pilgrim. Born Mildred Lisette Norman in New Jersey on July 18, 1908, for twenty-eight years she walked back and forth across the United Sates and Canada. In 1952, before taking on a cross-country walk, she was reported to be the first woman to walk the entire length of the Appalachian Trail in one season. About a year later, Mildred changed her name to Peace Pilgrim and set out on her first cross-country pilgrimage, from Pasadena, California. Peace Pilgrim did not walk with a group and carried practically nothing. In fact, her only possessions were the clothes on her back and the few items she carried in her small bag, which read "PEACE PILGRIM" on one side and "25,000 MILES ON FOOT FOR PEACE" on the back.

The athletic, blue-eyed, silver-haired woman vowed to "remain a wanderer until mankind has learned the way of peace, walking until given shelter and fasting until given food." She eventually died at the age of seventy-two; ironically, she was killed in a car accident in Indiana as a friend drove her to a speaking engagement. Though Teru and the other participants in the Global Walk did not plan to live as she did, Peace Pilgrim was a great inspiration to many in the group. She showed what was possible with the necessary trust and commitment.

When Teru set out on her journey, she had various intentions and motivations.

Like Peace Pilgrim, she wanted to spread the message of peace. Another motivation, similar to Gandhi's in the Salt March, was to make a statement and to help encourage a more ecologically focused direction for the country. Yet it was also an initiation of sorts for Teru, a chance to discover something inside herself—a greater sense of trust and courage.

In embarking on the journey, Teru was joining a long line of spiritual seekers, social activists, and adventurers who are called to the open road to test their abilities, learn about the world, make a statement, and discover more about their purpose and mission in life.

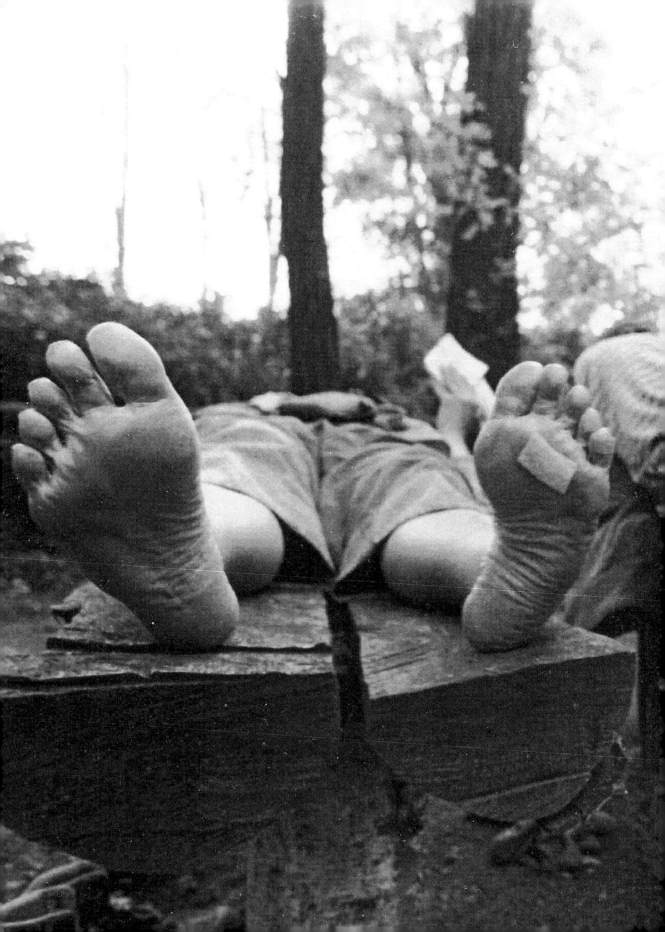

Lessons from Walking in the U.S.
Let Go of the Old to Enter the New

In the early weeks of the U.S. segment of the Walk, Teru felt very much at home among the hundred or so other activists. At times, though, she found herself mentally caught in her old life: she would look for her car keys when she no longer carried or needed them; think about what she should cook for dinner when it was no longer her choice but up to the work crew; and wonder if she had any phone messages, even though she had no phone and there was no way for friends or family to leave her a voice message on the Walk.

The Walk, she soon realized, presented an entirely new way of life, and to fully experience it she would have to let go of much of what she had become accustomed to—the ability to see her family regularly, to call someone anytime she got the whim, to go out for dinner with friends, or go to a store to buy her favorite treats. While she could easily do without the freeways and traffic jams of Los Angeles, other perks of the traditional American lifestyle were more difficult to give up.

She learned early on that the Walk was very much its own culture, with ways and customs unlike those of mainstream society: people usually paid little attention to what they wore; instead of gaining or acquiring things, the members of the group were dead set on making as small a footprint as possible; no one lived in a house or drove a car, so there were not the usual comparisons of wealth; and everyone had more or less the same position and vocation—they were walkers. In many ways, the Walk structured itself in direct contrast to the primary patterns of American culture.

When Teru was able to let go of her old life, she discovered that her new life had beauties and gems that weren't accessible in her previous one: she could spend evenings outside under the stars, telling stories and sharing tea with other walkers—people were not interrupted by a phone call or left a discussion to check phone messages. With very few means of outside communication, people could spend more quality time together. Her commute each day was no longer an hour ride in a car but a short walk from her tent to the road. And, unlike in Los Angeles, people were rarely in a rush to get somewhere.

Her first lesson was this: The more she thought about the pleasant aspects of her previous life, the more she missed out on the opportunities of the new life and culture. The more she lamented not eating the food of her choice, the more she missed out on the conversation at dinner with her fellow-walkers. The more she longed for the comforts of her home in Los Angeles, the more she missed out on looking at the stars with other walkers.

As a result, Teru resolved to be as fully present on the Walk as she could be. This was not the time in her life to spend her evenings watching cable television, going out to restaurants, or talking on the phone. She had lived that life and could do so again at another time. For this journey, she wanted to know and experience all that the Walk had to offer. And to achieve that she discovered that she had to let go of the old to enter the new.

A Livable World Stew

A second lesson that Teru learned early in the journey was that although people can sign up for the same endeavor, they can have vastly different reasons for doing so. This was particularly true on the Walk, which included people with diverse perspectives, all of whom had joined to help create a "livable world." There were adamant feminists, who blocked off an area in the camp each night for a "womyn's section"; hardcore earth-savers, who could quickly spout the most recent statistics on global warming and species loss; the diet-conscious, who were often vegan (consuming no meat or dairy) and viewed environmental change as occurring mainly through diet choices; "simple livers," who carried their own backpacks because they did not want to support oil companies by having their gear transported on a fossil-fuel-powered bus; deadheads, who focused on free expression and tended to drum much of the day (and night!) with no real interest in walking or learning about environmental issues; the health-conscious, who were interested mainly in the vigorous lifestyle that walking provided; and peace activists, who felt that no environmental change mattered as long as countries possessed nuclear weapons. All these subgroups, and more, signed up for the Global Walk for a Livable World, many of them believing, usually unconsciously, that other members would share their views. Teru described some of the diversity this way: "There were vegan gamblers and 'raw fooders' who would raid the kitchen truck after hours. Each group had its own ways."

While everyone was in favor of a livable world, Teru learned that this was the easy part; it was in the details that the rubber hit the road. "How could someone eat meat and still say they support a livable world?" some in the diet-conscious faction believed. "How one could support environmental awareness and not have the dismantling of all nuclear weapons as the No. 1 priority?" a good number of the peace activists thought. Each subgroup tended to believe that their particular vision and corresponding actions were most important to creating a livable world.

As Teru got to know the members of her new community, she was a little surprised at how varied people's views of a livable world were. She also could not understand certain subgroups, such as the members who preferred to drum rather than walk, and who seemed uninterested in educating themselves about environmental or peace issues. In the beginning, she looked at these members and thought, "How is what they are doing creating any kind of livable world? They have no place here."

Soon, however, Teru realized that no one faction on the Walk was completely right, and no one was really wrong. She came to see that the varying views of a livable world were in fact an advantage, for they led to diversity and rich dialogue. The movement toward a livable world had room for them all, from the "simple livers" to the diet-conscious to the peaceniks and even the deadhead drummers.

She discovered that what mattered most was not that everyone had the same views but that people supported one another to do their part. Together, through a mix of ingredients, the group could put forth a vision of a livable world that was not just focused on one action or a single ingredient but included a broader variety. A livable world, she realized, was more like a rich stew than like a single dish.

The Real Difficulty

The actual challenges that Teru faced on the U.S. segment of the Walk were significantly different from what she had imagined. Before the journey, she believed that walking roughly fifteen miles a day would be the most difficult part of the journey. She thought that enduring blisters, sore legs, fatigue, and changing weather conditions would make Walk life challenging at times and excruciating at others. After a few months, however, she discovered that while the walking did have its trying times, particularly on very hot days or in powerful rainstorms, on most days it was enjoyable and she had little problem keeping up with the others. She could walk at her own pace and there were always interesting people to talk to. Walking, for the most part, was quite pleasant.

What turned out to be more challenging was getting along as a community. This was the cause of great discord, partly owing to the attempt by the community to use consensus for all major decisions. Consensus was part of the livable world toward which most members aimed; they wanted to live in a world that was not ruled by representatives or controlled by the majority but was instead one where decisions were agreed upon by everyone. To accomplish this, though, took time and steady, patient effort. It often meant that conversations could go late into the night, if one or two people did not approve of a certain decision and no action could be taken until they did. Changing these people's minds, however, was not always the answer, since adjusting the plan so that those in the "no" camp would join the "yes" camp could make a few people in the "yes" switch over to the "no," creating yet another stalemate.

While consensus was an admirable ideal, with a hundred people it often resulted in endless discussions and, over time, in fewer and fewer people showing up for meetings, as they lost patience for the process. The community dialogues took much of Teru's energy. While she supported the process, she had not expected that a group would need so much time to make effective decisions.

Issues addressed at these meetings included whether to adopt a pig in the community which would eat food scraps and help reduce waste (this was tried, but later discarded); whether drummers (usually the younger ones) should be able to drum in the late afternoons, when other members (usually older) enjoyed napping; how to raise more funds to keep the Walk afloat; and how to handle members who broke the walker agreement by using drugs or who were not working as required. The group sought to make sure that everyone's voice was heard and that every member agreed with a particular decision. This was noble . . . and tiresome.

Teru discovered that living together as a community and relating to the other members was much more work than walking fifteen miles a day. This turned out to be just as true when she walked with a much smaller group in Europe and Asia. It was the interpersonal relationships that mattered the most and took the greatest energy.

New Ways of Seeing

A turning point for Teru occurred one day in Missouri, when she took cover from the rain in the office bus. She was drenched, as if someone had just dumped a large bucket of water on her head. Once inside the bus, all alone, the sound of the rain hitting the roof was like a bell of mindfulness at a Zen temple. The moment came alive. She enjoyed the sounds and smells of the rain coming in through an open window, then looked out the window to see walkers running for cover from the rain, some going to their tents and others heading for the buses. In this simple event, Teru felt a great ease and tranquility. There was a knowledge that, in her words, "the world was perfect." Nothing was out of place. Though she was all alone in the bus, she felt a profound sense of camaraderie. "In that moment," she wrote, "I couldn't remember ever feeling such joy to be a part of a group."

This moment opened a door in Teru, one of deep appreciation and joy. She knew, then, that the Walk was exactly where she needed to be. She was reminded of her motivation for the journey, and remembered herself as a four-year-old girl, distraught and confused about life and war.

At first, Teru questioned what in this quite ordinary scene made it so profound. So what if it was raining and people were running for cover? This happens all the time. As she pondered the situation, she concluded that the difference was not in the event itself but how she was viewing it. A door of perception had opened in her, so that she could receive such a simple event in a completely new way. The clarity of her awareness made the moment alive and wondrous.

It was then that she realized to what degree the Walk's lifestyle was affecting her. Spending all day outside, living so closely to the earth and the elements, she was becoming attuned to the cycles of life in a way that she had not known before. She realized what a gift this lifestyle offered. This deepening of her awareness and the connection to her environment led Teru to trust that while the Walk was grueling at times, it also offered a wealth of exquisite and unexpected gifts, as long as she had the patience and the perseverance to continue.

The Bigger World of Curiosity

Early on in the journey across the U.S., Teru noticed that locals whom the group passed generally responded to the Walk in one of two ways—with either curiosity or fear. The latter was expressed once when the Walk was passing through a small town in New Mexico, near the Texas border. Most of the locals, on seeing the hundred-strong band of dirty, earthy walkers marching through their town, believed the group to be not only odd but dangerous. They quickly hurried into their homes and closed their doors. This was the first time that Teru had witnessed a large group respond to them with such fear.

Though there were, to the eyes of many rural New Mexico residents, some "unusual-looking" walkers—one male walker wore only skirts, several people had long dreadlocks, and others dressed in very colorful or torn clothes —no one meant any harm, and there were also walkers like Teru, who looked and dressed like good old-fashioned clean Americans. Still, faced with a hundred people, an assortment of painted school buses, and feral-looking trekkers carrying earth flags, some locals could not appreciate the rich diversity of this unique band. Though people generally knew very little about the Walk's mission, it was clear that the walkers were "different," and this fact alone was enough to keep many locals at a safe distance. As the principal of a school in a nearby town told them some days later, "You frighten many people in our community."

The same feeling was expressed one day in rural Missouri, when two male walkers noticed an elderly woman alongside the highway trying to fix a flat tire. As the two men jogged across the road to help her, the woman took one look at the young, shirtless walkers headed her way and, with the quickness of an N.B.A. guard, threw her tools on the ground, jumped back in her car, and sped off as fast as she could—that is, as fast as a person can drive with a flat tire. Many who witnessed the event laughed, but it was a reminder of just how often the group scared people.

This was an important lesson for Teru. She saw how fear can limit one's experience, and how much more opportunity there was in acting out of curiosity. For those who approached the group out of interest and openness instead of fear, there was much to gain. With these people, Teru shared stories from her journey, discussed environmental solutions, and listened to the issues and concerns they had. Usually, in such interactions where people engaged with a willingness to learn, everyone left feeling enriched.

Teru often wondered why many locals, encountering a hundred fascinating people walking right by them, chose to hide instead of to engage. Much of the reason, she decided, was a fear of the "other," of those who looked different or acted in a way that was outside the norm. Rather than complain about this, Teru took it as a lesson, and made the decision early on to go toward instead of away from those whom she viewed as different, whether it was a harried businessman in a three-piece suit or a rifle-toting cattle rancher.

Commitment as a Reminder of What's Important

Something that Teru hoped to learn more about in her journey was commitment. She wanted to understand better how to put her full mind and heart behind a cause. The issue most dear to her was the impact of nuclear weapons, particularly the destruction caused in Hiroshima and Nagasaki. It was paramount, she believed, that this catastrophic event serve as a lesson. Before the Walk, she often wondered what she could do to honor the friends and loved ones who had died or become sick as a result of the bombings, and to make such an event less likely in the future.

Her solution was to educate people about the devastation that resulted from nuclear weapons, and, more important, to help others recognize the great bond that exists between all people, no matter their culture, race, or belief system. It is when we forget the underlying connections we have, she believed, that people can treat one another cruelly. As long as we know and feel what binds us together, we really can inhabit a livable world.

As an expression of this commitment, Teru had decided to carry the Hiroshima Peace Flame on the Walk. To her, the flame represented both the destructive power of people and the hope for a better world. An offshoot of the flame had been transported to Los Angeles from Hiroshima before the 1984 Summer Olympics, and it was kept at various temples and other locations in Los Angeles. Teru obtained the flame, and bought a red foot-tall hurricane lantern in which to carry it.

Keeping the flame lit on the U.S. Walk took constant work and attention. She only purchased the baby jogger after the U.S. segment, so on most days she arranged to have the flame transported to the next site on one of the buses. She kept it in her tent at night, and when she had to leave the Walk to do a chore she asked one of the other members to take care of it. The tending of the flame took great vigilance, for if it ran out of lantern fuel or was knocked over it could easily be extinguished. So Teru had to always keep track of where it was and how much fuel it had.

Before the Walk, Teru often viewed commitment as something of a chore. But caring for the flame, although it took sustained attention, was also a great gift, for it was a continuous reminder of her purpose in walking every day. Each time she looked at the flame glowing in the red lantern, she remembered her dedication to peace.

She learned that, when commitment is a reminder of what is important, even when a task is time-consuming and challenging it is also a gift. Of deciding to carry the flame on the Walk, she said, "Carrying the Hiroshima Peace Flame provided a marvelous mode for self-discovery and a reminder of the goodness of all people. It was a constant reminder to believe in people, to trust that peace lives in the hearts of all people."

When in Doubt, Cheer

"Get a job, you damn hippies!" screamed a man in a slow-moving green car as the walkers made their way across the George Washington Bridge from New Jersey to Manhattan, on their last full day of walking on the U.S. phase of the Global Walk for a Livable World. With his window rolled down, and his car moving at about five miles an hour, the man continued to yell obscenities at the group. "Go to hell or wherever you came from!" he continued, shaking his fist out the window. His voice increased in volume and intensity with every word he spoke. In the group's nine months of walking, no one had ever directed such intense rage at them. People had expressed doubt and anger and at times hurled a bottle or two, but no one had verbally attacked the group so vehemently.

Teru and the others continued to walk, unsure of how to respond to such hatred. Then someone in the back of the group had an idea: he started to clap.

Soon others joined in. Then a walker began to cheer, and then another, and another. The clapping and cheering made its way to the front of the group, until soon a hundred-person roar rose up in response to the man's insults. "Yippee!" one person shouted. "Hooray!" another added.

The man continued to scream at the group, but the cheering was so loud and forceful that it drowned him out. People could see his fist shake and his lips move, but his words could not be heard. Now it was the man who seemed confused. This was certainly not the response that he had expected. He soon sped off, and was never seen again.

Teru was touched by this event, for it was not with anger and hatred but with applause and celebration that the man was silenced. The man had provoked the opposite impact from what he had intended. Instead of being made to feel hurt or ashamed, the walkers were energized by the interaction. They entered Manhattan with smiles on their faces and joy in their hearts. The man had, quite unintentionally, reminded them of their ability to meet hatred with joy.

This was an important lesson for Teru; she realized that if they had responded to the man with similar hatred they would have given him what he wanted. The event showed Teru the power of not reacting with hatred or aggression to insults coming one's way. From this point on, Teru knew that when one is insulted and unsure what to do, the most effective response may be to cheer.

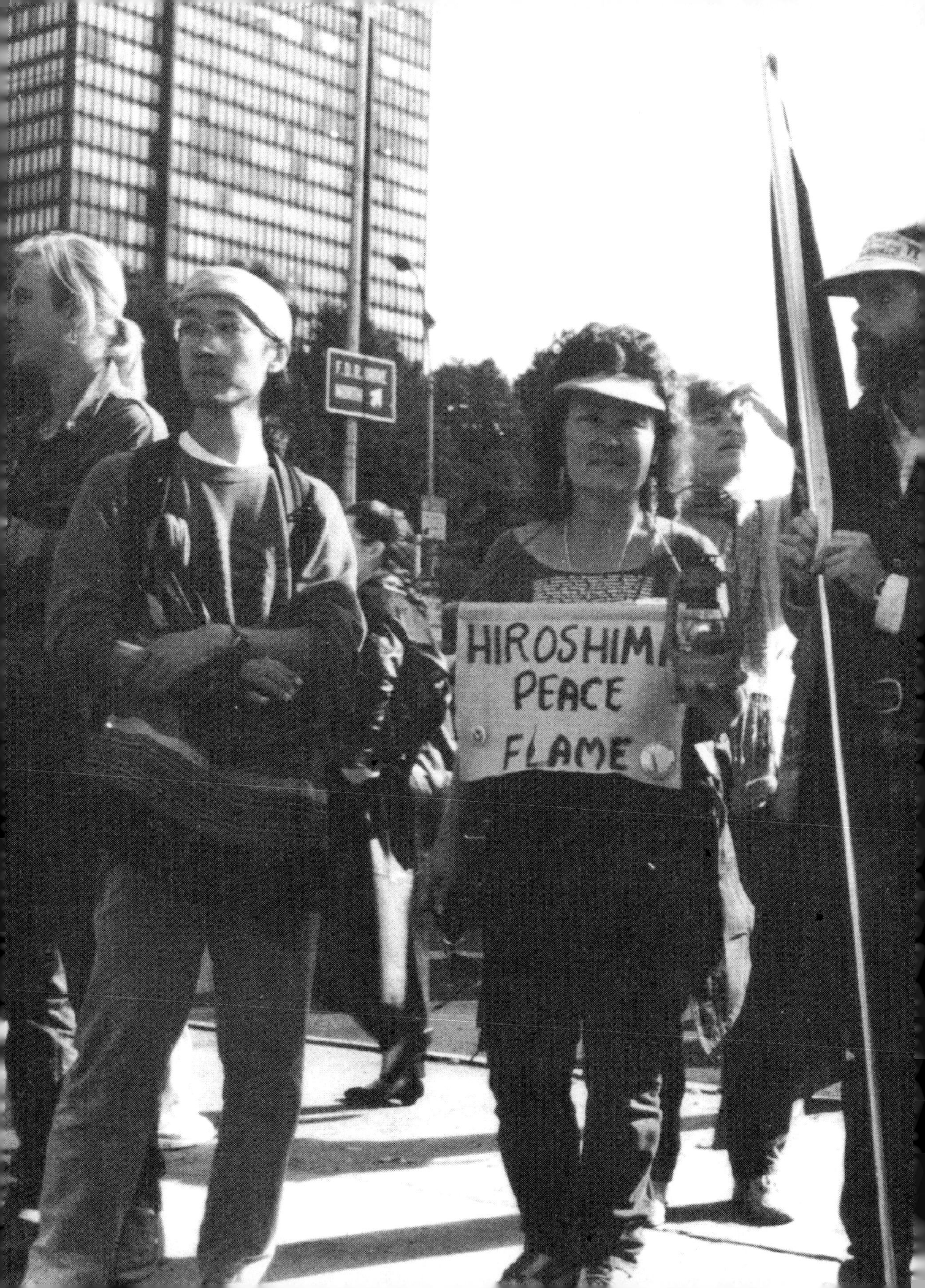
HIROSHIM
PEACE
FLAME

New York City

Teru stood across the street from the United Nations, in New York City, wearing dark jeans, a purple short-sleeved shirt, and green hiking boots. In her left hand, she held the lantern that carried the Hiroshima Peace Flame. It was early afternoon, the first week of October, 1990, and the day was clear and sunny, the air slightly chilly. Teru and nearly a hundred others had just walked, accompanied by a police escort, from where they spent the previous night, at the Cathedral of St. John the Divine, on the Upper West Side of Manhattan, to the United Nations, in midtown, on the East Side. They had arrived at their destination.

Teru looked around, occasionally chatting with the man next to her, a peace activist from Japan who had come to meet her at the closing ceremony of the U.S. phase of the Global Walk for a Livable World. With walkers and supporters surrounding them, the two enjoyed the festivities. Though the group's journey was ambitious and long, the closing event was nothing fancy, since by this time few in the group had the energy or the will power to organize anything grand. A band played on a small stage, and refreshments were provided. Teru observed walkers embracing family members, while others exchanged hugs and addresses as they prepared to go their separate ways.

It had been an exhilarating nine months for Teru since she had left Southern California. She had walked more than 3,000 miles, a feat that, at the beginning, she doubted she could accomplish. The trek had taken her from the Pacific Ocean through the flat, open Mojave Desert; to the welcoming Native American reservations in the Southwest; along the dry, windy terrain of the Texas Panhandle; through the gentle hills of the Ozarks in Oklahoma and Missouri; into the forested Appalachian Mountains in West Virginia; and, finally, to the urban sprawl that extends from Washington, D.C., to New York City.

Teru was especially grateful for the outreach that the Walk had made possible. It allowed her to meet new people, from farmers in Texas to Quakers in Pennsylvania to inner-city kids in Philadelphia. In big cities and rural towns, Teru spoke to peace groups, churches, schoolchildren, and community organizations. To initiate discussions, she often told the story of the Peace Flame, explaining how it symbolized both the destructive capabilities of humans and the hope for a better world. She was always impressed by how the presence of the flame was able to focus and deepen conversation.

Nine months was a long time to live in a tent and be without the comforts of traditional society. It was not surprising, therefore, that on completing the journey across the U.S. most walkers were ready to hang up their walking shoes. Some were returning to college, others to their jobs. Some were not sure of their destination, but they knew one thing: they would live somewhere other than a tent.

While most were preparing for their post-Walk life, Teru felt that her journey was just beginning. The group was called the Global Walk in the hope that at least a few members would continue beyond the U.S., but there was no set plan to do so.

In the previous months, meetings had been held about a possible continuation across Europe and Asia, but these were not well attended and few people expressed any interest in venturing through foreign countries, where the walking would be more difficult and there would be few, if any, support vehicles.

Standing at the closing ceremony, Teru looked around the group, wondering who might continue the journey with her. She saw Joan, the Walk's visionary and its key organizer, but she knew that Joan had never planned to continue beyond the U.S. and was already planting the seeds for her next project: a large eco-village near Ithaca, New York. She then saw Greg Edblom, from Eugene, Oregon, who had become one of her closest friends and walking buddies, but he was unsure whether his body was up for such a journey. Other people in Teru's age group also had concerns about whether they could physically handle such a trek. The twenty-something walkers, on the other hand, though generally more physically able, were noncommittal. When Teru had asked them about their level of interest, they had usually responded, "Maybe we will come to Europe. Sounds cool. I don't know now. Let's just see what happens." Teru knew this group was too young and responsibility-resistant to commit to, much less help her organize, such a journey. However, if she started it, she was hopeful that some of the younger walkers would later join her.

As she considered who might go with her, Teru wondered how she would begin to prepare for a Walk that would take her through countries where she knew no one and did not speak the language. In the U.S., she understood the culture, and the group had an array of support vehicles, from a kitchen trailer to a refrigerated truck. For the Walk to continue beyond the U.S., it would have to take a completely different form. Just how this would look she was not sure.

Can I go it alone? she asked herself, after she was unable to locate many possible Phase II members. Can I really walk through countries such as Yugoslavia, India, and Cambodia, where I do not know anyone or speak the language? Teru could not answer these questions, but she sensed in her legs and her heart the strength to continue the journey, somehow, some way. The journey was not over for her; she had more walking ahead.

A few days later, Teru flew to her parents' house, east of Los Angeles. There she unpacked her things, rested, and tried to figure out how she would walk across Europe and Asia—all while carrying the Peace Flame. Still the questions persisted. Can I really do this? Am I crazy? Where will I sleep at night? How will I carry my things without the support buses we had in the U.S.? Where will I get food without a kitchen trailer and a refrigerator truck? And how will I carry the fuel and other supplies for the flame?

Teru considered her options, including buying a van that would follow her on the journey, carrying her luggage and food and also possibly providing a bed. She decided, however, that this would be too expensive and cumbersome. She could get sponsors to help pay for such a vehicle, she supposed, but she wanted to walk, not spend her time fund-raising. More important, she sought to use as little technology as possible, so people in poorer countries would be more likely to engage with her. She wanted to travel relying on people's kindness, not the latest technology. Furthermore, a vehicle that she had to raise the money to buy, find someone to drive, fill with gas, and fix when broken seemed like a tedious chore that in the end would only add complexity to her journey.

But if she did not have any support vehicles, she asked herself, how could she continue across Europe and Asia? There as not really anyone that she could call for advice. Many had walked across the United States, including members of the Great Peace March, a few years earlier, and Peter Jenkins, whose 3,000-mile trek across the country was chronicled in his books A Walk Across America and The Walk West: A Walk Across America 2. However, few had attempted to venture beyond the U.S.

While at her parent's home, Teru contemplated the details she would need to work out. First, there was the issue of transporting her belongings. She needed both the basics, such as clothes and rain gear, and also fuel, charcoal, and a lantern to keep the Peace Flame. With the extra material needed for the flame, Teru decided that the best means of transporting her belongings would be not to carry them on her back but to push them on wheels. One way to do this, she surmised, was to use a three-wheeled racing jogger. Such a vehicle would make walking much easier on her back and allow her to bring more than what she could carry on her own.

The jogger would, however, present its own challenges, such as the need to carry patches and new inner tubes for flat tires, and would restrict her to paved roads, since she would be less free to take routes across uneven terrain. And the jogger could also hold up her journey if it broke down. Even considering these downsides, Teru concluded that it was her best choice. To test out the idea, she went to her local sporting-goods store, bought the first jogger she saw, and took it home. A few days later, she wrote "Los Angeles, 1990 to Hiroshima, Japan, 1993" on a yellow cloth, tied it to the top of the jogger, and prepared for the journey. She would later call the jogger her "strolley."

Food and housing, however, were not as easy to solve. The three-wheeled strolley would help carry her belongings, including a tent, but she still needed a place to set up the tent at night and a means to get food along the way. She also had questions about her safety: What if I got sick or hurt? How can I navigate in foreign countries where I do not know the language? Can I really do this?

These issues could not be solved by a trip to a sporting-goods store. Teru realized that these questions were essentially about trust. Could she trust the universe to provide what she needed in so many different countries? This was the question she had to answer, for there was no way that she could organize all the details of where to stay and what to eat in countries such as Greece, India, and Cambodia. Besides, once on the road, she knew that her route could easily change, and that she might need to bypass some countries altogether.

It was not a question of money, or the right kind of gear, or adequate maps; it was one of trust. Leaving her job and her home for months to participate in an organized Walk with a hundred others, accompanied by support vehicles, across a country that she knew well, had already required some level of trust. But venturing by herself or with a few others across lands like India and Pakistan —this required a something else. She asked herself whether she could live with such trust in the universe, and was surprised to hear a small voice inside her forcefully answer the question: "Yes, you can do this. Go." Her body tingled with excitement, and energy filled her legs. Teru knew then that one way or another she was going to keep walking across Europe and Asia. To do so, she would need to rely on the goodness of people across the world to provide what she needed.

During the months following the U.S. Walk, she sought out others who might join her. Writing to a friend, Teru tried to spark her interest by sharing the possible highlights of such a trip: "Join me in this trek," she wrote, "and we will listen for our echoes in the Himalayas, sample Reishi mushrooms in China, watch the sunset from an Indian temple, and eat our way across Japan." She continued, much like Walt Whitman in *Song of the Open Road,* "There are lazy muscles to work out, tents to use, expanding waistlines to trim, and slippery money to deal with. Come on!" She argued, "Three years is not that long a time, really."

In the end, none of Teru's close friends shared her enthusiasm. Walking for years through foreign countries, carrying or pushing one's belongings in heat, snow, and rain, was not most people's idea of a good time. But Teru was happy to learn that one other walker from the U.S. segment, Carolyn Latierra, wanted to continue the journey in Europe. Carolyn was a longtime peace activist who was about Teru's age, and Teru was thrilled that Carolyn would be with her. On March 28, 1991, roughly six months after the U.S.

Walk ended, Teru and Carolyn flew to London to make their way by foot across Europe.

Once she and Carolyn began the Eurasian phase, it did not take long to gain another member: Birgit Mertens, a twenty-four-year-old German woman. Birgit had traveled to England from Germany seeking her next path in life, not knowing where it would lead. When she met Teru and Carolyn in England and learned of their journey, the idea of walking through Europe for peace and the environment struck a chord. She knew that the Walk was what she was looking for, and quickly joined them.

Lessons from Walking in England, Holland, Poland, and Germany
Confronting Fears

The first lesson that Teru learned on the European segment of the Walk was the importance of confronting her fears. She was out on the open road in a way that she had never been before, without the comforts of the U.S. Walk and the benefit of even one support vehicle. She, Birgit, and Carolyn were completely at the mercy of their environment; if the weather turned bad or someone tried to rob them, they would have to rely on their wits.

At the time, she wrote down in a notebook some of the fears she had in embarking on this stage of the journey. Her list included: "Physical safety, getting lost or robbed, running out of water and food, not being accepted, making mistakes, looking bad, being ridiculed, and getting in harsh conflicts." But she took a positive approach toward these situations; the Walk was an opportunity to address fears that had always lingered inside her but that she had so far been able to keep at bay. She later wrote, "It was my good fortune on the Walk to face these fears every day!"

In fact, the process of confronting her fears started even before she took her first step on the journey. She wrote, "From the very beginning, by deciding to join the Walk, I had to let go of my home and family ties, and quit my job. It was scary. I felt like I was making a great leap into an abyss. I wondered to myself: Is it possible for a 51-year-old woman to just take off and suspend the familiar, the safe, the secure lifestyle that took years to accomplish?"

As the Walk progressed, Teru had to confront deeper and deeper fears, which had to be released in order for her to experience the journey fully. This involved giving up her home for a tent, living outdoors, and walking unprotected in foreign countries. Every day there were risks of some kind for her and the group—whether to trust the person who approached them, whether to walk in an area where there was danger or strife—in addition to the regular uncertainties about food and shelter. Amid such challenging conditions, Teru had a choice: either pull back in fear or do her best to confront it. She chose the latter, writing, "By taking risks, stretching my self-imposed limits, I got to release my fears. The payoff on the other side of discomfort and shaking is trust and strength—trust that the universe will provide all my needs, and the personal strength to follow my vision."

Teru knew that walking through foreign countries in the midst of many unknowns is both frightening and potentially liberating. The liberation comes only when one is willing to face fears and to call on a deeper reservoir of confidence. Teru decided to use the Walk as a means to confront her fears, and to discover what exists on the other side. Walking in Europe, she had never felt so vulnerable—or so strong. A confidence and a fierceness arose in her, and she resolved to do all that she could to follow her vision and walk with her friends just as far as she could go.

Fearlessness and Taking Three Breath

On the Walk, Teru discovered a practice that would help her better relate to her fears, which she called "taking three breaths." Anytime she noticed fear arising, she took three deep breaths. She claimed that this helped her to transform her fears and doubts into a kind of fearlessness, and, instead of feeling alone and prone to attack while on the side of the road, she could walk with power and confidence. She wrote, "Walking on the road with no guide or protection is a vulnerable place to be in; but it can also be a power place, a place to become more self-confident." To Teru, it all depended on the perspective and approach of the walker. It did not matter how strong or weak she was; what mattered was whether she approached the unknown with fear or confidence.

Teru discovered that in taking three breaths she was able to get more room around fear; it was not as all-encompassing as it once was. As this happened, she found that other qualities could more easily arise that were stronger than fear. She wrote, "I learned that my curiosity and propensity for adventure were greater than the frightening thoughts of new cultures. This fearlessness soon became more and more accessible as I trusted and relied on it." Rather than trying to get rid of the fear, she simply focused on other qualities, like curiosity, and knew that as those became stronger the fear would lessen.

When she was able to do this, she could act from a place of trust and confidence. She wrote, "Taking three deep breaths before diving is a part of living in fearlessness." This practice, she explained, would not make fear instantly vanish. That was not the point. She described the process this way: "Fearlessness is not the absence of fear; fearlessness exists in the presence of fear. They can occupy the same time and space. I am able to feel afraid and still act with courage. Fearlessness is to feel the emotion and dive anyway. And the more fearlessly I act, the more it becomes reinforced as my reality."

The Walk gave Teru regular opportunities to put this into practice—some nights she was unsure where she and her companions would sleep, other days strange men approached them, other times cars sped by, almost hitting them. But Teru always made it clear that one never knew the results of one's actions. All one can do, she claimed, is to act from the highest place; the rest was up to the universe. She said, "I take three deep breaths, shake some, go ahead and dive in, and trust that whatever the outcome is, it will be all right."

The Mission of the Walk in Europe

While the group in the U.S. often held "Livable World Fairs," showcasing alternative earth-friendly technologies, and gave talks in churches and schools on this subject and others, Teru knew that the Walk in Europe and Asia would likely not have the same opportunity for outreach. In the U.S., the group often knew in advance where they were going to be and when, so they could plan accordingly. A van was also available to transport walkers to community centers and other sites to give talks. This made it possible for Teru to meet with a peace group or a community organization when she was in town.

Outside the U.S., though, the group would travel without a schedule and with no support vehicles. Teru realized that the group's outreach and education would have to take another form: it would involve not just groups of people in specially arranged events but every person they met. To this end, the walkers would need to focus on "living" their principles and staying open to the opportunities for engagement.

In a letter to potential new walkers for the Eurasian segment of the Walk, Teru included this vision of the journey.

We will walk as pilgrims for the Earth

Students Learning

From the intimate encounters

We have with the people

And the land.

We will carry with us our belief that

We truly need to walk our talk

As activists for peace and ecological wisdom.

Person-to-person we create the

Friendships which will lead to

Authentic Security

A Livable World for us all.

Teru knew that the challenges of the Eurasian segment (with no set places to stay, no support vehicles, no phones or other means of communication, and often no common language) presented an opportunity to focus not on "events" but on "walking their talk." This, in fact, is always what mattered most to Teru. She realized that the best outreach and education was not just spoken but lived.

Receiving Help

It is possible to venture across much of the world without needing the kindness of the people who live where you're traveling. With enough money and planning, you could have an assortment of vehicles, resources to stay in nice hotels and guesthouses, and hired help to cook meals and carry supplies. If you had sufficient funds, you wouldn't need to depend on the kindness of other people. This would be one way to travel. It was not the way of the Walk.

Even in the U.S., when the group had support vehicles, each night they needed a place to sleep, and depended on the generosity of a farmer, a church, or a community center to provide a room where they could lay their sleeping bags or a field where they could pitch their tents. However, it was in Europe that the kindness of strangers was truly put to the test. The group traveled on foot, carrying all their supplies, and needed help of various kinds: places to sleep at night, directions to the next town, knowledge about where to obtain food and water, and much more. While members had some money with them to spend on food, they had to be very frugal. They might be able to afford to buy one meal a day, but not three, and no one had enough money to regularly stay in hotels.

For Teru, needing help was part of the beauty of the Walk, and it was what allowed the walkers to traverse unscathed through so many countries. She wrote afterward, "We needed the help of strangers in order to survive and, strangely enough, our needing their help for the basics of life diminished much of the trouble that might have otherwise come our way."

Teru believed that walking through a country unprotected and unafraid of the people brought out the best rather than the worst in those they met. Locals were drawn to help not because the group was protected and had everything they needed but because they were out in the open, unguarded, and accessible. Had they hired bodyguards or carried the latest high-tech gear or traveled with a state-of-the-art bus, they would have put up a wall between them and the people. She believed that this would have only created more division and encouraged potential robbers. Instead, Teru claimed, it was actually safer in most situations to be vulnerable.

Teru explained her approach this way: "Being out on the road in a foreign country, with only a backpack, at the mercy of the elements, drew people toward us in a way they otherwise would not have been. They easily saw our humanness, our struggle to endure and survive. For people who are very poor, it gave a chance to give. Many graciously offered us their field to sleep in for the night or let us fill our water bottles from their faucet. Such giving is so simple, and so profoundly enriching to both sides." When we trust locals, Teru believed, they are more apt to live up to that trust.

The Angel of the Day

Although almost everyone who approached the group was well-meaning and helpful, Teru claimed that one person usually stood out on account of great generosity. In Europe, she coined a phrase for such people: the "angel of the day." Somehow, she thought, these angels knew just when the group needed them the most. It was as if the walkers were sending out signals that these angels would pick up. She could not explain it any other way.

An angel could take many forms: a farmer in England might walk out on a scorching-hot day to greet the group with cold drinks; a poor villager in India might offer shelter to the group in a torrential rainstorm; a group of nomadic Afghan sheepherders in Pakistan might offer a tent to sleep in for the night; a doctor might offer his services for free to help a sick walker. Such expressions of kindness, often when verbal communication was impossible, were so common that eventually it no longer surprised experienced walkers. Teru would just smile and say to herself, "This must be our angel today."

This is not to say that there weren't trying times, or moments when the group needed help and none was available. But very often an angel did appear. For Teru, this deepened her trust in both the goodness of people and the wisdom of the universe. She was on the lookout each day for an angel, and most days she was not disappointed. As Teru liked to say, "If you expect such a person, you are more likely to recognize the person when he or she appears."

Fueling Stations

While the group occasionally took trains or planes when necessary, on the vast majority of days they used almost no fuel. There was no need to stop at a gas station, since they traveled on foot. The only vehicle they had was Teru's strolley, which she pushed. However, while fossil fuels were rarely used, Teru and the others relied on another type of fuel—what they gained through their interactions with locals.

The people whom Teru met every day on her journey provided the fuel to keep her going through hard times. She wrote, "I was touched and impressed by people everywhere I went. Seeing courageous, independent women leaders in India, dedicated peace and environmental activists in Europe, compassionate and generous villagers in Eastern Europe, and people in the Third World countries making do with what they had reinforced many of those traits in me. Meeting dedicated peace activists and openhearted villagers gave me the strength to continue on my journey when it was hard and frustrating. In those times, I thought about the enormous care and love of the people I had met. It was this feeling of care and connection that often kept me going."

Most of these people did not provide anything specific; it was the simple act of engaging and giving that energized Teru. This was one of the greatest "renewable resources" that Teru found herself using on a daily basis. The local people she met were her fueling stations, the places she could visit to get recharged.

Some days, children provided this fuel. She wrote, "I remember children looking at us with amazement as we walked through their village. Although we did not always converse with them, seeing us on the road often sparked a kind of excitement and fascination in them. Sometimes the children would come running up to us to touch our faces or give us a small gift. Because we were so unprotected on the road, we were more accessible to the children. They often could not hold back their curiosity; they had to make some kind of contact. It was so encouraging to interact with them, even when we did not speak their language. Their beautiful, young, fresh smiles said so much."

In this way, Teru relied on a type of renewable energy to keep her going, one that came from her daily interactions.

Attending to Emotions

It is often easy to act skillfully when conditions in our lives are pleasant. When we are sitting in the comfort of our home after eating our favorite food, we are more likely to respond with ease and clarity to a challenging event. If someone is angry with us, and we are relaxed and well nourished, it is easier to respond calmly. However, when our situation is difficult—we are hungry, wet, or exhausted—responding skillfully is much more challenging.

While the Walk had its share of pleasant experiences, it also had its share of unpleasant ones, and in these times Teru learned to be particularly attentive to her emotions. There were periods when it rained for four days straight and every item she owned was drenched; or the group was out in the countryside with no homes or stores nearby, and had to go to bed hungry, after eating only a piece of fruit for dinner; or they took a wrong road and had to backtrack for miles to get to their destination, walking thirty kilometers that day instead of twenty. It was in these times, Teru knew, that it was easy to act out of frustration and anxiety.

Teru often said that the greatest challenge in any endeavor, including spending years walking, was not physical but mental. It was attending to one's emotions and acting from ease instead of from stress. Of course, the blisters were painful, the weather conditions could be grueling, and the terrain was often unforgiving, but much of this was bearable if one was in the right frame of mind. In a nervous or agitated state, a ten-yard walk to the end of the street can be excruciating. In the right frame of mind, a three-year walk can be immensely enjoyable. For the latter, Teru believed, one has to be both mentally and physically prepared. Part of this "mental preparedness" was learning to attend to one's emotions. When we are controlled by our emotions, Teru claimed, and we unconsciously act out of fear and anger, we serve neither ourselves nor the world.

For Teru, this meant trying to better understand strong emotions such as anger.

In moments of great emotional crisis, she sought to skillfully "release" such feelings rather than let them simmer or explode at people who were not the real cause. To help her relate to the flood of emotions that arose while on the Walk, Teru often relied on a process called Re-evaluation Counseling, which she had been trained in before the Walk. Re-evaluation Counseling, or co-counseling, is a method in which one person helps another by giving open attention and helping the person release negative or distress patterns through talking, thus freeing up the emotions—what co-counselors often referred to as "emotional discharge."

To do this, Teru sought support from fellow-walkers, such as Carolyn. Teru described one such situation: "One day in Western Europe when I was furious, my fellow-walker, Carolyn, helped me get into my anger and let it out. I beat an old daybed while Carolyn supported me. I hit that bed so hard that dust filled the room like fog. With her support I was able to work through my anger. Only after letting myself go into those emotions could I again focus on the events of the Walk with an even state of mind."

Teru knew that keeping an "even state of mind" was essential to her survival. She found again and again that when she lost this she paid the price. Teru wrote, "One day in Holland, I was so upset at another walker that I was not watching my step while going to my room inside a beautiful old mill. I took a tumble and hit my right knee. The pain was so bad that I cried. That situation was ripe for an accident. And I did it to myself; there was no one else to blame. I could not blame it on the person I was angry with. I had to miss a few days of walking. This experience made it clear that I had to take care of myself if I wanted to survive the Walk."

Skillfully addressing her anger and frustration was just as important, if not more so, than having the right kind of clothes or gear. Disappointment, anger, fear, anxiety— these, Teru said, were the blocks to surviving the Walk.

What the Walk Was Like

Many people asked Teru what it was like to spend three and a half years walking across the world. She said, "Rather than tell people about the experience, I try to take them there." What follows is, in her own words, her attempt to "take people there." I am leaving her words and descriptions just as she wrote them.

"Imagine you are in another country. You don't know the language, you have no map or dictionary, you only know you are going east, and you need directions, food, water, and shelter for the night. Remember, no one can understand a word you say. What do you do? Do you freeze with fear? Do you let the unknown take you over? No, you start making connections with people the best way you know how. You use hand signals, you show pictures to help communicate ideas or needs, you act things out, you do whatever it takes. You connect with the person you are talking to on a human level. They love that you are struggling to communicate, that you are trying to speak their language. When you do this, the atmosphere becomes light and fun. You tell them who you are and what you are doing. We often told people: 'We are peace walkers from the USA and we are glad to be in your wonderful country.' Through making this kind of contact, we would find a place to sleep, a store for a map and dictionary, and food and water.

"When you see fear as a challenge, rather than something to run from and try to avoid, it can call forth your creativity. People will see a certain strength and integrity in you that will draw them towards you. So much opportunity opens up when you are not controlled by fear; when you see it as a challenge, as an opportunity to bring out more of yourself.

"One of my first challenging opportunities to face fear was upon entering Poland. None of us spoke Polish, we had no dictionary, no map, were low on water, and had heard stories of the extreme poverty there. Even though we were enjoying the exhilaration of entering another new country, we soon got anxious upon discovering that there was no bookstore in the town we were in, and that most of the city was closed. We continued to walk through the city until we reached the city limits.

"Finally, at an intersection, we decided to flag down one of the few cars on the road. The first person who stopped was a nervous and suspicious looking man. Since he had to stop for cross traffic, we stood in front of his car and knocked on his window to make contact. 'We are peace walkers from the U.S. and we could use your help,' we said. The driver conversed in German with Birgit, and let her know that he had just emerged from the forest and didn't want to be bothered. He turned out to be a smuggler, dealing in illegal cigarettes. We laughed afterwards, but we were very vulnerable out on the edge of town and he could have easily harmed us.

"We still did not know where to go or what to do next, but we had to keep going east. We knew that we had to be creative and rely on our resources. So onward we went asking a few more people until we found someone who gave us some water and food. A little later, we saw a roadside café, with a little wash bowl in front and handmade picnic tables around the yard. We saw chickens running in the yard and wondered if they served eggs. Not knowing how to ask that in Polish, we flapped our arms in a squatted position screeching Bawk-Bawk, as we attempted to imitate a chicken laying an egg.

"The workers laughed, and knew immediately what we were trying to express. These friendly people later directed us to the next town where we found a place to set up our tents for the night. Through relying on our creativity, we found food to eat, and, maybe more importantly, had an enriching and playful interaction with the workers.

"This experience in Poland helped give me confidence that I could trust my creative skills. As I continued the Walk, I found that the more I trusted and relied on my intuition and creativity, the less afraid I was and the more people were drawn to help me on my journey."

The View from the Road

Teru often spoke of how life looked different while walking and living on the road. A new fancy car that can easily cruise at a hundred miles an hour may look impressive in a showroom and be fun to drive, but, when it zooms past a walker a few yards away on the highway, that car is not so pleasant. It is just a big object that causes a great deal of noise. Instead, Teru said, it was the simplicity and beauty of things that mattered most to her while living the walker's life. She found herself appreciating cars that drove slowly and the unique characteristics of a well-made house or building.

To her, many of the new buildings, fast cars, and expansive homes of developed countries, while impressive, distanced us from one another, adding traffic and using unnecessary resources. A smile from a person riding a bike was much preferable to cars whizzing past her; she enjoyed engaging with the owner of a small shop in an old building rather than one in a giant store with many employees and intense lighting. It was in this stage of the journey that Teru began to see that in our effort to "modernize" we often lose more than we gain. From walking on the side of the road, it was the little things that mattered most.

Teru said that on the Walk she learned to view life from a slower rhythm. By doing so, the speed at which many cultures operate, particularly in Western civilized countries, felt hurried and rushed. When she lived this lifestyle in Los Angeles, it seemed normal, but, when she stepped out of it and viewed society from the road, the pace of our modern world appeared incredibly, and unnecessarily, hectic.

She was not always sure what to do with this new awareness, and did not judge those who lived as she once did, but she did often wonder what a culture would look like that prioritized a slow, quality, non-rushed lifestyle. From her experience on the road, this was far richer and more enjoyable.

Budapest, Hungary

Teru sat at the kitchen table in a small apartment in Budapest, Hungary, loving the Walk lifestyle and wondering why she had ever doubted whether it was right for her. It had been a thrilling four and a half months since leaving London on foot. The Walk was fairly organized in England, since Teru had a contact there, and she and Carolyn and Birgit found themselves welcomed with open arms everywhere, often hosted by various peace groups. She was deeply moved by the kindness of people who housed and fed them. When asked at the time about their good fortune on the journey, Teru insisted that it was not luck that made it possible; it was alignment. She claimed, "It's not luck or fate. It's more. We are a part of a whole, a circling energy that brings to us as we give. . . . I am always amazed." In her early weeks in Europe, it was this synchronicity that most impressed Teru.

From England, the three women traveled to Holland, and Teru arrived there in high spirits, excited to meet again a Dutch woman named Diane van Leeuwen, who had walked across the U.S. with the group. Largely owing to Diane's efforts, they were treated like royalty throughout the country. Every day, a local walked with them, and they were offered food and shelter each night, supported by a variety of peace groups. They were mentioned in a dozen newspapers and were interviewed on five radio stations. The Walk was turning out to be everything that Teru had hoped, and more.

After Holland, they continued to West Germany and East Germany. In East Germany, Teru was impressed by the humility and simplicity of the people, but she was saddened to hear of the frustration and hopelessness in the young. With Birgit as a translator, Teru was able to have many discussions with people living in this country, which was in the process of reunification and had, only a few years earlier, witnessed the falling of the Berlin Wall, which had separated East and West for twenty-eight years.

East Germany was the first very poor and underdeveloped country that Teru had visited on the Global Walk. Writing to a friend at the time, she said that her first impressions were "WOW. How fortunate I am to be here." It was a time of rebirth for the former Communist country, and Teru had concerns that it would simply copy the patterns of the West.

Over all, the first few months on the road in Europe had been thrilling. Writing to a friend at the time, Teru described her experience this way: "I am on the highlight of my life trek, this once in my life dream come true." The weather was bearable, people were kind and welcoming, and she found that pushing fifty pounds on her strolley was not that difficult, as long as she stayed on paved roads. And, most important to her, she was able to show people the Peace Flame and talk about it everywhere she went.

She said that she wanted to yell to the people, "Don't let them kill the beautiful and wonderful parts of your villages! Do you really need shopping malls, asphalt streets, and more cars? Do you? Please reduce, recycle, and reuse. Keep your wonderful cobblestone streets, spacious gardens, and bicycles and trains for transportation."

At this point in the journey, Teru had seen many large shopping malls, which had replaced family-owned stores, and new housing developments built over old ones. In this kind of "progress," she felt, the unique aspects of a place get lost. She did not want East Germany to follow this pattern, and talked to the people about the importance of keeping their traditions and culture alive while they modernized.

While in Budapest, Teru received more good news when four new walkers, friends with whom she had walked across the U.S., joined the group. One of them, Essrea (who went by the name Ess), was a twenty-eight-year-old native of Rochester, New York, who had been on the entire U.S. journey. Petite, with curly brown shoulder-length hair and lean, strong, toned muscles, Ess arrived with great enthusiasm. She had first heard of the U.S. Walk while working at Arcosanti, an intentional community in the high desert of Arizona dedicated to alternative home design. Arcosanti was along the Walk's route, and an advance team visited to inquire if the walkers could stay at the center for a night on their way through Arizona. Ess was working as a waitress in the restaurant there, and had no idea that the group was on a cross-country walk. She could not understand why the handful of straggly twenty-somethings she was waiting on ordered only water. When the group got up to leave, one of the walkers handed Ess a Global Walk flyer, and invited her to join. When she read the group's mission statement, Ess knew instantly that this was for her. Like many others, she had heard of the Great Peace March across the U.S., and had been on the lookout for a similar walk that she could participate in. Now a group representing the Global Walk for a Livable World was standing right in front of her.

Ess arrived in Budapest with a friend from the U.S Walk, twenty-one-year-old Abigail Bokaer, the daughter of Joan Bokaer. Abigail had long brown hair, a slim build, and, like most walkers, a zest for adventure. When Abigail learned that Teru and Carolyn were on their way across Europe, she contemplated meeting up with them but did not seriously consider it, because she did not have the necessary funds. When Abigail mentioned to a friend her desire to join the group in Europe, she was shocked and elated when the friend offered to sponsor her on the journey. Abigail no longer had any good excuses not to join, and she prepared to meet the group in Europe.

Around this time, Ess visited Abigail in Ithaca; once she learned of Abigail's plans, she thought, "Heck, if Ab can do it, so can I. I would love to join the Walk in Europe." But there was a small problem: Ess did not have the money and knew of no potential sponsor to cover her trip. Seeking a creative solution, Abigail and Ess spent a day discussing fund-raising options. They remembered that there were hundreds of leftover Global Walk T-shirts that could be sold to raise money. Abigail and Ess soon went door-to-door and manned booths at farmer's markets, gathering donations and selling the T-shirts to raise the necessary funds. After four to six weeks of work, they succeeded. As a result, Ithaca was awash in people wearing Global Walk T-shirts, and Ess had enough money to join the Eurasian segment of the Global Walk.

Abigail wrote Teru a letter to one the Walk's contacts in Europe, who passed it along to Teru. Teru wrote back suggesting that Abigail and Ess meet Teru and the others at a hostel in Budapest called the Hotel Lido. They took a cheap flight to Spain, and in true walker fashion they were going to hitchhike from Spain to Budapest, but after hours standing by the side of the road, with no one even slowing down, they had to give up and take a train. Fortunately, they arrived at the hostel just in time to meet up with Teru, Carolyn, and Birgit.

Along with Abigail and Ess, two other members also appeared at the hostel, much to the group's surprise. The simple-living duo of Taz and Star had spent the previous few weeks hitchhiking through Czechoslovakia looking for the walkers, not knowing that their initial route had changed. Months before, when they learned that the Walk was continuing in Europe, Taz and Star wanted to join, but they already had plans to bicycle from Chico, California, to South America, with no particular country or destination in mind. After two weeks, however, they decided to ditch their bikes and instead walk and hitchhike down the southern coast. They arrived in southern Mexico just in time to experience a total solar eclipse, then continued to Belize and Guatemala. Seeking a larger community with which to travel, they left Central America to find the walkers in Europe, earlier than they'd planned.

Taz and Star were consummate travelers. When I first met them, on the U.S. Walk, they were getting out of an eighteen-wheeler after a long hitchhiking trip. Each were carrying a few bags of sprouts, which was their dinner that night—and many other nights. At the time, they chose to eat only raw food, avoiding anything processed or cooked, which meant any grain (unless it was sprouted) and all bread, dairy, and meat. Taz confided in me at the time that he would occasionally "binge" and eat a yam, but this was rare. Needless to say, the two took simple living quite seriously.

They argued that if everyone ate only raw food there would be no need for packaging, and the world's trash would be reduced by millions of tons every year. It was hard to argue with them, but it was even harder to follow their example.

Taz and Star flew to London, then hitchhiked east, first to Czechoslovakia, then to Budapest. As the exemplary simple-living couple, they arrived with no tent, and small packs, each of which included a poncho, a journal, toiletries, one change of clothes, and a glass jar big enough to sprout garbanzo beans in. Since winter was approaching, everyone else had tents, sleeping bags, and warm clothes. On arriving in Europe, Ess's and Ab's packs weighed about fifty pounds. This may be light for a person out for a weekend camping trip in the woods, but for walkers carrying their packs every day it was quite heavy, and both Ess and Ab quickly began shedding many of their belongings after a short time on the road.

Raised by a professor father and a schoolteacher mother, Taz had excelled in academics as well as sports. Disenchanted with college and seeking adventure, he traveled to Armenia, which had been hit by a devastating earthquake, to help build houses with Habit for Humanity. He then decided to travel much like a pilgrim, inspired in large part by Peace Pilgrim. This eventually led him to the Global Walk. Teru was particularly happy to see Taz in Budapest, because in many ways he reminded her of herself when she was younger— adventuresome, carefree, and not afraid to try new things.

Star, a few years younger than Taz, was born and raised in the northern Sierras by parents who were committed to an alternative lifestyle. As a child, she had spent most of her days outdoors, learning from an early age how to grow and harvest food, get water from a creek, cook with a wood fire, and make and sew her own clothes. Star's ancestry was Norwegian, and she had been a long-distance runner in high school; in many ways, she had been raised outside traditional culture, and the Walk was, for her more than for most others, similar to her upbringing. She used as few resources as possible and kept her blond hair short, cutting it with the scissors of her Swiss Army knife.

Teru enjoyed her time in Budapest, as she was able to rest and catch up with old friends. Afterward, the group of seven headed south, toward Yugoslavia, where the violent conflict between the Serbs and the Croats was under way. Teru was energized by the presence of the new members and the support they had received so far in the journey. She left Budapest with great enthusiasm.

Lessons from Walking in Hungary, Bulgaria, and Yugoslavia
What You Seek May Be Right Next to You

Every day on the journey, the group had needs to meet, specifically food and housing. For these, the group often relied on help from locals. Some days, food and shelter were easy to come by; at other times, such as on desolate stretches in the country, there were very few options and they made do by sleeping in fields and eating local fruit for dinner. Often the best way to find food or a place to sleep was to ask people in the area, most of whom were more than willing to do what they could.

Though people were generally extremely helpful, pointing the group toward a grocery store, offering them a meal, or letting them sleep in their house, sometimes what the walkers needed could not be found by asking for help. Sometimes what the group sought was in fact right next to them.

This became clear one day when the seven decided to split up to look for free housing while in Budapest. They had stayed the previous nights at a hostel, but since they wanted to spend more time in the city and had limited funds, they sought cheaper, preferably donated, housing. So one person stayed at a local park and watched everyone's belongings while the rest scoured the city in groups of two.

The Walk had been blessed with free housing for most of the four and a half months in Europe. Just about every day, housing had appeared in one form or another: inside a church, at a generous person's home, at a train station. They expected the same opportunities to arise in Budapest. The pairs walked for miles across the city, visiting every church and community center they came across, peering inside abandoned buildings looking for possible shelter, and asking shop owners. Even with all their efforts, they couldn't locate a place. All three groups returned to the park, shaking their heads in disbelief. (They later found out that the Pope was visiting, which may have had something to do with the lack of options.)

However, while not one of the teams searching the city could secure housing, on arriving back at the park, the housing problem had worked itself out, in a way none of them had expected. A man named Nick had looked out the window of his apartment, which was by the park where the walkers left their belongings, and had managed to make out the sign on Teru's strolley—the yellow cloth over the handlebars that read "Los Angeles, 1990 to Hiroshima, Japan, 1993." Curious, he came down from his apartment and walked over to the group. "Are you on some kind of peace walk?" he asked. When the walkers said that they were, he said, "Well, if you need a place to stay, my apartment is right across the street. I would love to have you stay with me." After searching for hours in every corner of the city, the housing for that night appeared right across the street from where they had started.

Teru always smiled at such occurrences, for they were lessons in how the universe often works in mysterious ways. It reminded her that what you are seeking could be right next to you—or at least just across the street.

Go the Opposite Direction

The Walk taught Teru the importance of not following the masses, and that at times she needed to do the exact opposite of what everyone else was doing. In many ways, the group was already going against the tide. While other people traveled by car, plane, or train, she and the group went primarily by foot. While most people were trying to build their careers, the walkers had no real vocation except making it from one place to another each day. While most people planned their days, Teru and the group moved from one place to the next having no idea what would happen or where food and shelter would appear.

The importance of going in the opposite direction was made apparent when the group entered Yugoslavia, which at the time was experiencing a volatile war between the Serbs and the Croats. As the walkers approached the border from Hungary, they witnessed miles of cars waiting bumper-to-bumper to leave the war-torn country. Many cars were loaded to the brim, filled with people's most precious belongings, as they did not know when it would be safe to return or

whether their homes would still be intact when they did. People had suitcases and TVs tied to their car roofs, clothes stuffed in front of the rear windows, and trinkets of all kinds lying across dashboards. It was uncertain at the time how fast the violence would spread, and people wanted to get out of the area before it escalated. Looking at the people leaving, Teru saw frightened expressions, and she wondered how it must have been for her family to pack up their belongings when they were sent to internment camps during World War II, when she was a young child.

Though there was a long line of cars waiting to get out of the country, there was, not surprisingly, no one besides the walkers trying to enter it. Had the walkers only been concerned about what other people thought, they would have followed the masses and immediately made a U-turn and headed back the way they had just come, believing that everyone attempting to leave must know something they did not. Why go one way when just about everyone else is going in the opposite direction?

While people likely had good reasons for leaving Yugoslavia, it didn't matter to the group, which had already decided to walk in the country as long as officials would allow them. Teru never second-guessed that decision. She knew that doing the exact opposite of what everyone else did could, at times, be a very good sign.

Go Naked: Simplify

Most people were shocked to discover how little Teru and the other walkers carried on their journey. No one had a cell phone to call for directions, and often not even a guidebook of the country in which they walked. In fact, as the Walk progressed across Europe, Teru carried fewer and fewer possessions. She called such an approach "going naked."

She said of her journey, "One of the important lessons I learned on the Walk was simplicity. I first learned this on the U.S. Walk, when I had to trim my

belongings down so that they would fit in a small gear space on one of the buses. We had another vehicle that carried our tents and sleeping bags to the next site. When the Walk got to Europe, we no longer had the help of a vehicle. This forced me to get rid of everything except the absolute essentials: a change of clothes, rain gear, a notebook, and sometimes a tent and a sleeping bag in the winter. I quickly learned that the less I carried, the easier it was on my muscles."

All the walkers tried to find ways to minimize their belongings. Taz and Star, two of the true minimalists of the group, pared down their belongings so that their packs weighed only five pounds. They started with store-bought backpacks, and later created their own smaller, homemade packs. Then Taz, not wanting to carry a jacket and a sleeping bag, created a jacket/sleeping bag so that he could essentially have one warmth-providing piece of material that could be used day or night. He did this by sewing together the sides and the bottom of two blankets, which was quilted with fabrics that friends had sent him for the journey. He then cut out a small diamond in the middle so he could also wear it as a poncho. He later gave up his homemade backpack and just rolled all his belongings in his poncho/blanket, tied it together with some string, and slung it over his shoulder. People he met, not believing you could travel with so little, often asked him, "Where is your backpack?" They could not believe that he rolled up all his possessions and simply slung them over his shoulder.

At fifty years of age and with a flame to carry through Europe, Teru could not live with so little, but she continually asked herself during the journey, "What do I need and what can I let go of?" Her goal was to discover what she truly needed, and to let go of everything else. She later wrote, "Of course I needed certain possessions, like my strolley to help me carry the Peace Flame and rain gear to keep me dry from rain, but anything more than the basics only weighed me down."

While simplifying made it easier on her muscles, for Teru it also provided a lesson in trust and self-sufficiency. She wrote, "Simplifying allows one to act with integrity and determination—knowing that you have only what you need and nothing more. Discovering this increases a person's self-confidence."

Be a Global Student

Though Teru was very comfortable telling people about her journey, she wanted her listening skills to be as honed as her speaking ability. When she entered a country, she was as much a learner as she was an educator. While she was happy to share her wisdom, she was more interested in helping bring forth the wisdom of others. She wrote, "There is no way you can enter another country and tell the people about peace. You can only open up the subject and encourage dialogue. Peace is not something one person learns, then preaches to everyone else. It involves discussion: making the space for everyone to be heard. It takes each one of us being willing to both share our truth and listen to others."

Teru thus made a concerted effort to be a learner, and to listen as much as she spoke. Of course, language barriers prevented this on occasion, but she knew that, as a guest in another country, her primary role was that of student. She had to be open to learning the culture and the customs of the places she went. She wrote, "Entering a new country, there is so much you do not know. And, when something is unfamiliar, fear easily becomes the driving motivator. When fear is the motivator, new territory and people are seen as a threat to your beliefs and ways. You feel that you must protect yourself and your beliefs. When this is the case, you can easily appear domineering and obnoxious to the people you meet, as you attempt to protect and defend your ways."

When visiting foreign countries, most people stay at hotels and take guided tours, and often have little actual contact with the locals. For Teru, such contact was paramount. She wanted to meet people with different worldviews and have her beliefs questioned. Teru welcomed dialogue that could change her thinking. She wrote, "Most people in lesser-developed countries only see Americans through a car window as they speed by their area, or when they serve them at one of the resorts. Rarely do they get to meet them as equals, invite them into their homes, and share stories and experiences."

This was not easy, particularly in parts of the world such as northern Pakistan, where many people had an unfavorable view of the U.S. Instead of responding with fear, Teru was fascinated to learn more about why they held such views. She wrote, "It takes trust and willingness to make contact with people of different cultures. You must be aware of the beliefs and mannerisms you bring into a culture and how those may be viewed by others. Your body movements, the tone of your voice, your eye contact or lack of, are read by people according to their culture and background."

This is challenging enough in one country, and even more so when entering a new country every few months. Part of what helped Teru and the others trek from one country to the next was entering as students, and trusting that if they were open to learning then the lessons and knowledge they needed would present themselves. Teru often talked about the Walk as one big classroom, and the curriculum for her and the other "students" was learning from whatever happened on a given day.

Happily Crazy

Another question that Teru was asked both during and after the Walk was how she was able to survive on the road for so long. People wanted to know what it took for her to perform such a feat. During an interview in northern Pakistan, she responded to this question by saying, "I think it takes being a little crazy. Not the kind of crazy that puts me into an institution, but the kind of crazy that is far-out curious and impractical."

She encouraged all of us to follow our vision, regardless of what others might think. This, to her, was living courageously. Of course, Teru encountered skeptics throughout the journey, people who thought the Walk was fruitless, stupid, or simply silly. They did not believe that one person could make a difference or that walking around the world carrying a flame would help anything. On seeing her push her strolley down the road, like a homeless person, while carrying the Peace Flame, which looked like any old flame you could get by lighting a match, there were people who thought, "What a nut! Is she crazy?" When such phrases were verbalized to her, Teru was apt to respond, "I am crazy. Happily crazy."

What mattered to her was that she was following her vision; how others viewed her mattered less and less as the Walk progressed. In fact, she claimed that one of the most important elements needed in order to complete the Walk, or to do anything visionary, was caring more about one's vision than about what other people might think of you. So, while some people viewed Teru and the walkers as crazy, it was a label she was happy to have.

The Walk taught Teru to take praise and blame in stride. She did not try to convince people that she was any different from how they viewed her. Some people saw her as a saint, others believed her to be an idiot. It did not matter, really. Her job was the same: to keep walking.

Honoring the Forces of Nature

For Teru, the Walk was also a lesson in appreciating nature more deeply. Before the journey, she lived a traditional American lifestyle, very much protected from the natural world. She worked indoors, where the temperature was controlled with air-conditioning in the summer and heating in the winter. She drove a car to work and slept in a comfortable home at night. Her life, as is the case for most Americans, was lived in large part unaffected by the weather.

The Walk changed all this. In spending almost all day outdoors, she was thrown into intimate contact with the natural world—the wind, the cold, the heat, the wetness or dampness of the air. From such direct contact, she developed a greater appreciation for the forces of nature. She wrote, "Nature is  completely amazing and unpredictable. Out on the road with only a backpack, you realize how vulnerable you are to the powers of Nature. I was humbled by its immense power."

Before the journey, Teru thought fondly of the natural world, and enjoyed hiking in the mountains or spending a day at the beach, but whenever the weather turned unpleasant she would quickly retreat inside. This was usually not an option while walking. Through such direct and consistent contact with nature, she discovered that "nature is not always pleasant and sweet. She can also be harsh, with extreme heat, blistering snowstorms, or torrential thunderstorms. But the power and strength of nature is also a call to awaken and to respect the mystery of the natural world."

It was just this kind of respect and awe that Teru thought was missing in much of the world, particularly in First World countries. She said that people in modern societies easily forget to leave their house to enjoy a summer rain shower, to look at the stars and the moon at night, or to feel the intense wind before a storm. The more we live without such contact, the more we miss an essential beauty of living. In such a life, it is almost impossible to be in harmony with the natural world, since we do not know its beauty or its strength.

In fact, at times she felt sad for people who go for weeks without viewing a sunrise or the stars at night. "Out here," she would say, "you can't miss nature, because it is all around you."

Act Thoughtfully

While walking in Europe, Teru learned an important lesson about paying attention to one's actions and not acting immediately on impulse. She explained it this way: "One day in Hungary we were famished; we had not had anything to eat all morning. Usually we had some cheese, oats, yogurt, or even raw chickpeas to eat, but this day in Hungary we had nothing. There was no village for many kilometers; we were in the countryside, with no cafés or shops nearby, just cornfields and pastures. There were, however, wild elderberries lining the roadside. Star had mentioned that they were edible and sweet-tasting. Due to our great hunger, we took bunches of them, eating handfuls as we walked. Then it started: intermittent diarrhea and vomiting for the rest of the morning. It was as bad as the worst seasickness. Thank goodness for the cornfield. The green cover made for excellent privacy. We were not thinking when we stuffed the elderberries in our mouths. We let our hunger take us over. Had we been more attentive, we would have measured the situation first by asking a local person if the berries were edible. We went from being hungry to being sick."

Teru concluded from this experience, "When you are not mindful and you let your desires take you over, you often go from one ailment to another." She discovered the value of not acting strictly on impulse, and instead trying to see a situation clearly and then responding appropriately. Just because something looks and sounds good does not mean that it is right to act on it. She learned to assess each situation according to its long-term benefits.

Athens, Greece

Teru lay on a cot in a small cabin outside Athens enjoying the sounds of a thunderstorm, as the wind howled and heavy rain pummeled the roof. She and the others were staying at an alternative vegetarian health/nutritional retreat center, which had offered them a free place to relax for a month before they continued on their journey. As Teru listened to the rain, she felt a mixture of relief, fatigue, and excitement, as the group had just finished the European phase of the Global Walk.

Since Budapest, the group had traversed the former Yugoslavia, Bulgaria, and Greece. From Budapest, it had taken them about two and a half weeks to reach the border of Yugoslavia. Though the group had more than twice the number of walkers than they had in Western Europe, they had little problem finding adequate food and shelter, and often were invited into people's homes at night. For food, they were given bread and would "graze" throughout the day, enjoying the assortment of grains, fruits, and vegetables in the region, such as figs, apples, watermelons, corn, tomatoes, and grapes.

They arrived at the Yugoslavian border from the north, near the town of Szeged. At the time, members of the group were somewhat concerned about the level of violence they might encounter in Yugoslavia. They had been told that the war had not yet spread to the north or the east, so Teru believed that their planned route was relatively safe. Teru had agreed with the decision to walk in Yugoslavia, and she knew that if the war spread she and the others could quickly leave the country. For Teru, whose life had been so affected by war, it did not make sense for a peace walk to change its route because of a conflict, unless the group were in physical danger.

Once they took their first steps in Yugoslavia, Teru and the others were immediately struck by the kindness and generosity of the people. They saw no signs of a country at war. In fact, had they not been told about the war they would never have known that it was going on. As they progressed, however, locals shared stories of friends and relatives who had been sent off to fight. Still, even amid the turmoil in the country, the group was treated with respect and hospitality, and Teru found the Yugoslavian people to be hardy, gregarious, and welcoming.

Though the people were friendly, just about every day the police stopped to question the group, at times escorting them to the local police station and releasing them only after the group had answered all their questions. This happened so often that after a week the walkers began to expect it. Initially, they didn't mind; the police were generally friendly and often offered them food and drinks at the station. In fact, local police stations became rest stops for the group, and they spent many afternoons eating and drinking tea with local officials.

After about three weeks in Yugoslavia, however, one police chief took a different approach. He was suspicious of the "peace walkers" he had heard about, and had his officers bring them in for questioning. After confiscating their passports, he made the group wait for hours while he discussed the situation with other officials. He then singled out Ess, summoning her into his office. Teru tried to join her, but the chief refused. He then proceeded to grill Ess about the purpose of the Walk in Yugoslavia; why Birgit, who was German, was with them, and whether they knew anything about her background; and what the people they met were telling the group about the war. Meanwhile, the rest of the group played around outside the station, painting their faces with watercolors, singing songs, and basically goofing off. Though the police chief seemed somewhat rough, they thought that their time at the station would end just like every other such visit had during the past three weeks: with a handshake and good wishes.

This time, however, was different. After making the walkers wait for much of the afternoon, the chief emerged from his office to announce that the group had twenty-four hours to get out of the country. He gave no explanation. From her discussion with him, Ess believed that his decision was largely a response to the walkers' ability to interact with and hear stories from locals about the war, and, since they were travelers, to spread that information to the outside world. Since the chief wanted to control as much as possible the information that left the country, he demanded that the Walk leave—and fast.

Teru was disappointed with this news, but there was not much she could do. There was no higher-up official to whom she could protest the decision, she did not have the phone number of the U.S. Embassy, to call and issue a complaint, and she knew of no judge who would hear her case. "Besides," she told herself, "he could actually be acting on our behalf," as she had no idea just how widespread the war was. No matter the real reason for the police chief's decision, the result was clear: the group had to leave Yugoslavia as fast as they could. After a quick group discussion, they decided to exit at the Bulgarian border. They could walk through Bulgaria and proceed into Greece, the last country on the European phase of the journey.

The walkers all used different methods to reach the border. Teru and Carolyn chose the most dependable means, by train, while the rest broke up into small groups to hitchhike. The younger walkers, particularly Taz and Star, would pay for transportation only when it was absolutely necessary. Being ordered to leave Yugoslavia in just twenty-four hours did not fit that category. In the end, however, they all made it out in time.

Bulgaria was the poorest country that Teru had visited. East Germany was destitute, but Bulgaria, which only two years earlier had broken its ties with the Communist system and the Soviet Union, was having even greater difficulty adjusting to the new way of life. In fact, only the previous year Bulgaria had held its first free elections since 1931, a remarkable event. However, the structures of the old system remained in place: there were long lines to buy bread, stores had almost nothing in them, and people were uncertain of their future. Still, Teru found the Bulgarians to have a down-to-earth simplicity that was similar to what she had experienced in East Germany. People were not caught up in material possessions or surface appearances, as she had witnessed in more affluent countries.

The group continued southeast through Bulgaria, eventually arriving at the border with Greece. They then headed directly south, to Athens, their final European destination. Going from Bulgaria into Greece was a shock. They had left a country in great poverty and entered one full of modern homes, new cars, stylish clothes, and what seemed like an unlimited choice of foods.

Now, on the outskirts of Athens, Teru was grateful to have made it, but she was also tired. As she lay on her bed, she knew that she needed to rest. She was worn out, not as much from walking ten to twelve miles a day or spending the last nine months trekking across Europe but from her role as the always available Walk counselor. While she was thrilled to have more walkers join and happy to be available to help people, the previous few weeks had seen an explosion of relationship issues, many of which required her immediate and focused attention. It was initiated in part by the breakup of Star and Taz. This set off a flurry of new relationships, with people getting together one week only to split the next. Through all this, everyone looked to Teru for guidance and support. It was a role that she was happy to fill . . . but it was exhausting.

Over all, Teru was still excited to be on the journey. Traveling from London to Athens had taken about nine months. Not bad, she thought. People had received them well, her legs were strong, and her will was steady.

By this point in the journey, Teru was starting to notice changes in herself. The walking in Europe was much more adventuresome and rugged than in the U.S., and the lifestyle required a deeper level of trust. To express this change, in Greece Teru changed her name. Up until this time, everyone knew her as Judy—this was her given name at birth. But at this point in the journey the name "Judy" no longer felt true to her. So she asked people to refer to her by her middle name, Teru, which in Japanese means "to shine."

She had already had many chances to make this change. In fact, on the U.S. Walk a number of people changed their names, often choosing ones that were more exotic or alternative: Spyder, Shanti, Peace Pilgrim II, Faith, and a host of others. Teru, however, never felt compelled to change hers at the time. After finishing the Walk in Europe, something in her had come forth, and she wanted to acknowledge this through a name change. The name Teru seemed more than appropriate, for not only was she trying to keep a flame alive for three years across the globe, she was also feeling a trust and a spirit in her that was beginning to shine more brightly.

To continue the journey from Greece to India, however, the group would have to find other means of transportation, since they were unable to obtain the necessary visas to walk overland through Syria, Iraq, or Iran— countries

that did not have good relations with the United States—to get from Europe to Asia. Teru knew before she left the States that the group would not likely be able to walk overland through these countries, and calls from Athens to the Iranian Embassy proved fruitless.

Because the group had to leave Yugoslavia suddenly, and had to make other changes to their route, they had reached Athens several months earlier than planned. They were not expected in Bombay for some time. As a result, the group took time off to travel in Turkey and the Middle East. Then they flew from Athens to Bombay in late January, 1992, to continue the Global Walk.

In Bombay, they gathered two new walkers: Mohammad Usman, a strong, dark-skinned Indian Muslim in his twenties, from Bombay, and Sawazuchi Shoni, a young, soft-spoken Japanese monk who was living at the Bombay temple at the time.

Lessons from Walking in India
Why Are You Walking?

People across the world were drawn to Teru and the other walkers. In many places, locals were shocked to see a group made up mostly of Americans trekking through their country with no support vehicles and little gear. While many people wondered how far Teru had traveled, how many shoes she had worn out, and how many countries she had visited, the first and most pressing question people usually asked was "Why are you doing this? Why are you walking?"

This was particularly true in India, which has a long tradition of peace walkers, the most notable example of which was Gandhi, who used walks to protest injustices such as the British tax on salt. The question "Why are you doing this?" came in both cities and in rural communities. It was a fair question and one that Teru was happy to answer, but she found it challenging, since she did not always know how best to express her reasons for walking, and the reasons changes at times. Early on during her trip, she usually responded to such questions by saying that she was walking to express her concern for the planet and to help create a more peaceful world. She would show people the Peace Flame, and remind them of the power and importance of living and treating others with respect.

Over time, however, this answer felt rehearsed and did not always express what was true for her in a given moment. She laughed one day in India when Ess was asked at a school what the Walk's message was and she surprised everyone, including herself, by responding, half-jokingly, "Don't worry, be happy." Teru appreciated that Essrea was able to express her "message of the moment." She also loved the story of how a driver in the U.S. pulled his car over to the side of the road to ask a walker this same question, and before the driver could do so the walker said, "Could you tell me why you are driving? I have seen all these cars going by today. Are you guys a part of some group trying to protest something?" Above all, Teru valued spontaneity and truthfulness, writing after her journey, "I learned that too many set answers often bore both the speaker and the audience."

What mattered to Teru was not finding the single best answer she could repeat to everyone who asked but to speak what was true "in the moment" and to connect with the person asking the question. She was as interested in learning about others' lives as she was in speaking about her own. In the later stages of her journey, when someone asked her why she was walking through their land, she often responded, "I have come all this way to meet you! Tell me about yourself."

Such a response at times resulted in a quizzical expression from the questioner, but more often than not, before too long, the person was smiling and engaging with Teru. In fact, what most intrigued and motivated her was people. She once said about her reason for the journey, "I walk to meet people and to better understand this wacky, amazing world of ours. What better reason to walk?" Walking, she would say, allowed there to be nothing between her and local people. "I don't have to pull over to the side of the road to say hello to someone or look at a sunset," she mused. "I spend all day on the side of the road. I'm already there!"

Rather than having one answer to why she was walking, Teru chose to see it more like a Zen koan, which has no set verbal answer; instead, through the repetition of the question, a person can reach a deeper understanding. Most days, one never quite knew what was going to come out of Teru's mouth when she was asked about the purpose of her journey. But, no matter the words she used, the result was the same: a deeper bond with the person asking the question.

Our Shared Bond

What inspired and nourished Teru on her journey were the seemingly ordinary experiences that most of us often take for granted. It was the everyday expressions of care and connection that brought a smile to her face and warmth to her heart. She claimed that these experiences were both ordinary and extraordinary. They were ordinary in the sense that nothing particularly special or momentous was occurring, and they were extraordinary in that they were expressions of what is basic in all human beings. She called this connection "humanness."

She explained it this way: "To watch children playing, a woman working in the fields with a baby on one hip and a tool in the other, the interaction between a father and his baby son, the pleased gleam in the eyes of someone who is helping us find lodging or food, the grief of a young Serbian woman over the death of her father . . . one encounter after another showed me the depth of our humanness."

As the Walk went on, Teru began to notice this basic humanness more often, and to trust it more fully. As she did, an interesting change took place: the more she saw this humanness in others, the more others noticed it in herself. Each reinforced the other. She wrote, "Over time, I knew I could count on this deep place in me, and therefore I knew that I could count on it in others, too."

Teru loved to marvel at what on the surface were quite ordinary events, and invited her fellow-walkers to share in them with her. It could be anything—a mother picking up a child, a man laughing with a friend, a teenager lending a hand to an elder. Such events were signs to Teru of our shared humanness.

For Teru, a big lesson of the Walk was that it is in the ordinary that we can find the extraordinary. The fact that people cared for one another and could act unselfishly was truly miraculous. The Walk taught her how important simple, everyday acts are. In fact, though she welcomed help of all kinds, it was not those who took the group out to fancy dinners who most impressed her. Teru appreciated any food or other gift, but she was also grateful for the little offerings: a smile, a cup of tea, or simply a wave as she walked by. All to her were reminders of our basic humanness.

The Walk's Most Prized Possession

If there was a most valuable material object on the Walk, it was a small pink book known as the" Walk Book." The book, about three inches by five inches and about twelve pages long, was put together by Teru, Carolyn, and Birgit early on in Europe, to help the group communicate with people who spoke other languages.

A big challenge of the journey was letting people know the group's needs— was there a restroom nearby, somewhere to get food, a place to sleep? Instead of trying to learn how to ask for these in all the languages of the world, the book allowed the walkers to point to a picture of an item. It was usually easier for someone to understand what the group needed through images than through a walker's attempt to speak the local language. The little pink book became an important communication tool, especially in India, where many languages are spoken.

The book included signs of animals with an X over them, to indicate that the group was vegetarian, and a page of things enjoyed by walkers, like a bath. It also explained the purpose of the Walk, with symbols of peace, a big red X over a picture of a nuclear missile, and ecological symbols such as trees and oceans. Along with this, the book included a picture of the group's route across the world. Using the book, in a few minutes a person could learn a great deal about the Walk without a single word being spoken.

Using Bollywood and Fans

The group was fortunate, on arriving in Bombay, to meet a politician, peace walker, and famous Bollywood actor named Sunil Dutt. None of the group, of course, had ever heard of him. However, they shared walking stories with him and had their picture taken together for a local newspaper in Bombay. They enjoyed meeting him, but didn't give much thought to the encounter. However, several days later the photographer from the newspaper caught up with the group on the outskirts of Bombay and gave them a picture he'd taken of the group with Sunil Dutt. "This may come in handy on your journey," he remarked with a smile. Essrea said that they had no idea at the time (1) how popular Bollywood movies were even in the remote regions of India, and (2) how beloved Sunil Dutt was. They would soon find out.

For much of the journey in India, Mohammad communicated with locals to help secure housing for the night. He would introduce the group as important peace walkers. But when Mohammad was not present or the group needed some extra "ammunition," all they had to do was pull out the picture of themselves with Sunil Dutt, which they kept in the Walk Book, and locals would jump with excitement. After an initial expression of awe, people would usually hurry to gather all their friends to see the picture of the band of walkers with this well-known actor. Afterward, the group usually had no problem finding someone to offer them housing for the night.

Of course, the walkers did not have their picture taken with Sunil Dutt in order to impress locals along their route, but since they had been given the photo, and it seemed to matter to locals, they used it freely. They viewed it as a gift from the universe to help them survive in what turned out to be one of the most challenging countries in which to walk. Teru always followed the principle to "use what you have," particularly if one was walking for a cause, as they were.

While having housing most nights in India was very helpful in keeping bugs at bay, it often did little to offer relief from one of the most pressing concerns:

the constant heat. Many nights, the temperature cooled off only slightly, and the walkers lay in bed still sweaty from the day's walk. This was a challenge for all the walkers, including Teru. Most nights when they had been invited into someone's home, Abigail, Essrea, and Teru were given a room in which to sleep, separate from the men. Rooms often had three beds and they would have to decide who would get which bed. It was one thing to walk in hundred-degree heat during the day, but it was another to try to sleep in ninety-degree heat with little chance of cooling down. In deciding where each of the three should sleep, the comfort of the bed mattered, but usually the biggest factor was the placement of it in relationship to the fan in the room. Though Abigail and Essrea cannot believe now that they did not regularly offer Teru, their elder by more than twenty years, the best bed in the room each night, at the time they were young and did not have such awareness. Instead, they often took turns choosing.

One particular night, according to Abigail, they debated for a long time where to direct the one fan in the room so that each person would get a little breeze from it. As they were about to go to sleep, Teru noticed that she was not getting enough of the fan's air and tilted it ever so slightly toward her bed. Seeing this, Abigail remarked, "Teru! What are you doing?" At this, a tired and hot Teru replied, "Just leave it alone, Ab."

Abigail said that, in all their years of walking, this was the most anger that Teru had ever directed toward her.

Interesting Characters

To many people across the world, the band of simple-living earth-savers from America who walked without much of a plan or a map appeared quite odd. Some could not understand why members were not back in their country making money. America, they thought, is the land of opportunity. Why are you here? People in Asia had all kinds of ideas about Americans, many of which came from television made possible by the satellite connections that were starting to spread across Asia.

Part of the purpose of the journey to Teru was to show people another side of America, to engage people on common themes of peace and sustainability that crossed international borders. While the group appeared odd to many, at times they met people who appeared odd to them, and this was true in India more than anywhere else.

During their time in India, they came across a man who claimed to have rolled (yes, rolled) more than 1,300 kilometers for peace. When the walkers did not believe him, the man brought out newspaper articles and pictures to prove that he in fact had rolled 1,300 kilometers for peace. What made it a "peace roll" instead of just your average thousand-mile roll, no one knew. But, in comparison, their walking seemed almost normal.

The Struggles of the World

In walking, Teru and the others came in contact with all kinds of suffering and injustice. Teru wrote, "The Walk gave me a chance to see countries very clearly. I saw firsthand the degradation of the environment by thoughtless tourism in Nepal, the erosion of self-respect and initiative in Bulgaria by Communism, and the corruption of the right to self-determination in Cambodia by their own Khmer Rouge and even the U.N. occupying forces." Almost everywhere she went there was struggle of some kind.

Though she witnessed great suffering, Teru chose to focus less on the severity of the challenges and more on how people were responding to them. She said that, while there was great misery in many places, it was amazing to see how people were rising to the challenges they faced. In fact, she said that it was in these difficult places that people were sometimes the most alive. "These areas that struggle with monumental problems are not hopeless," she claimed. "They are islands of people who know what must be done. I met them, talked to them, and we shared meals and stories together. It was heartening and inspirational to see people meet the challenges in front of them."

What Teru saw in these places was people standing up and speaking out for what they believed in. She thought that the real test in life is not whether or not one faces conflict or difficulty but how people respond to those conditions. She said that what most mattered is that people "follow their highest sense of right no matter what." If people are doing this, she trusted that they would be able to rise to any challenge.

Creating Change

Some people questioned how walking for three and a half years across the globe could do anything to make a better world. "What real change could this bring about?" they asked. They wondered if the time might be better spent on practical efforts, such as creating better solar panels or more fuel-efficient cars. For Teru, these were important activities, but not the most important.

Teru believed that our greatest strength was in working together in trust and friendship. From this, amazing results would come. When people did not work together, when fear and discord prevailed, then no matter how noble people's intentions were, no matter how much funding they had, and no matter the I.Q. of those involved, very little good would come from their actions. The problem was not a lack of technology, funds, or know-how. What mattered, she argued, was a sense of teamwork and togetherness. If the world's countries had better relations, and each one put 10% of its current military budget toward environmental and peace issues and worked together on these, then incredible progress could be made.

Teru wanted to show people that Americans really do care, that peace and sustainable living benefits us all, and that each of us is necessary to create the world we want. Of course, watching Teru interact with someone in a distant country—exchanging smiles, trying to communicate, showing pictures of her journey—it could seem like very little was happening. But, for Teru, one-on-one interaction was necessary to build a greater sense of togetherness and community. It was this kind of interaction that might inspire a kid in northern Pakistan to think positively instead of negatively toward Americans, or prompt a wealthy businessman in the U.S. to start asking how he could help, or give inspiration to a woman in Poland to keep on the path of democracy. This did not happen because Teru lectured to people; it happened through an openhearted exchange.

While Teru's actions did not look like much—she rarely spoke to large crowds or met with political figures—in her mind she was helping to offer what the world most needed. After the Walk, she wrote, "The Walk showed me beyond a shadow of a doubt that we are all connected to the whole, and that degradation in one part is felt in another. Equally so, uplifting movement in one place affects all other areas as well. When we see this clearly, we know the path we must choose."

Our Greatest Strengths

The Walk in Europe and Asia survived on scarce resources. Teru had saved some money for the journey and received income from a condo she rented out in Hollywood, California. The rest of the group, however, scraped by with much less, often helped by their parents or small donations. Still, the group had no budget, no grants from foundations, and no corporate sponsors. For the most part, they traveled with just enough money for food and basic supplies. While this made the journey very difficult at moments, Teru saw a positive side, as it allowed them to discover and rely on non-material resources.

Teru claimed that our real strength and greatest resources are not what we own or carry. We all need certain basics in order to survive, but more important than these are the qualities that direct our lives. She wrote, "I learned that while the physical things we have or carry are important, it is the qualities of strength, courage, and trust we have developed that are our best resources."

Ironically, when one's inner resources are strong, she believed, other needs are more likely to be provided. In the right state of mind and focus on one's true inner resources, the outer ones are more likely to work out. For example, Star, during her time in Eastern Europe, traveled without a blanket. Since it was winter, every night she relied on someone to loan her one so she could stay warm at night. Because she was so outgoing, friendly, and trusting, she generally had no problem finding someone who was willing to loan her a blanket. Teru believed it was Star's friendliness and trust that made this possible.

Teru summed it up after the Walk by writing, "Walking lightly, trusting the unknown, you realize that your most priceless possessions come from inside you."

Wakefulness

An important lesson that Teru learned on her journey was the value of what she called "wakefulness." She wrote after the Walk, "Every moment is important and unique. To fully take in all the sights, sounds, and smells while walking, we had to stay in present time, in the moment. This meant freeing myself of thoughts that pulled me from this moment, from the 'now.' "

For Teru, the Walk was an opportunity to open her senses, to see and experience the world completely. The environment, she claimed, was continually beckoning all of us to wake up. She said, "The morning sunrise, the smell of sage, the call of crows, the sight of a large maple tree, all speak to us, saying, 'We are here. Look at us.'"

Without this quality of wakefulness, she would miss the beauty of the places she visited. Describing the need for and benefit of this quality, she wrote, "What good is it to walk through a beautiful European countryside when one is daydreaming or worrying about where one is going to sleep that night? If you are not present with your experience, you miss out on everything. The Walk showed me the importance of staying with my direct experience—my foot touching the ground, the wind caressing my face, the golden brown of a field."

She recalled one time when this quality of wakefulness was particularly strong. "One early morning in India, our troupe of five was walking before the sun had risen. Due to the blaring heat of India, we were often on the road before the sun came up. It was a very dark and cool morning as we walked out of a boys' school towards the village. As we walked, I could not help but notice the magic and beauty of the morning. Mysterious, flickering fires for morning tea lent coziness to the whole scene. As we got closer to the village pond, the sounds grew increasingly intense. I heard a rhythm of crickets chirping, frogs croaking, roosters crowing, birds singing, peacocks calling, and dogs barking here and there. All getting louder and louder, until the first sign of dawn. I fancied lifting right up off the ground and dancing to the crescendo, so thankful to be a part of it all. It was nature's magical orchestra for me. I felt such joy to be alive, and so thankful that I was present enough to enjoy it."

Living with wakefulness meant bringing her attention from the array of fears and hopes to her direct experience—her feet touching the ground, the sights and smells around her. Without this quality, someone could walk for years through numerous countries and only partially experience the beauty of the environment and the people. Teru put it this way: "Being present means absorbing everything around you and inside you. When you can do this and are alert to your environment, it helps you think more clearly and behave naturally." She said that the Walk taught her the truth of Thoreau's statement "Only that day dawns to which we are awake."

Delhi, India

Teru sat in the back room of a Japanese Buddhist temple in Delhi, India. The temple, a converted house in a posh neighborhood north of the city, was owned by the Nipponzan Myohoji, a group of Japanese peace-activist monks from the Nichirien sect of Buddhism. Teru was happy to have a chance to unload her gear and get a reprieve from the extreme dry Indian heat. She leaned back against the wall and took a deep breath. The previous two months had been by far the most difficult of her journey, and possibly her life. It was clear that for her to continue she would need to regain her strength and resolve.

Several months earlier, the group, which included Teru, Essrea, Abigail, Taz, and Star, had arrived in Bombay by plane from Athens. In Athens, two members left them: Carolyn returned to the States, and Birgit went home to Germany. The plan for the others, once they were in India, was to walk from Bombay, in the south, to Delhi, in the north, a distance of roughly 900 miles.

None of the group had ever traveled in India before and they were not prepared for the challenges that lay ahead. Perhaps Teru had been overconfident, having walked three times that far across the States, and the equivalent distance through Europe.

After landing in Bombay, Teru prepared for the upcoming trek. She met with contacts, conducted media interviews, bought lighter clothes, obtained extra inner tubes for her strolley's tires, had her trusted Teva sandals repaired, and planned the route between Bombay and Delhi. Mohammad Usman and Sawazuchi Shoni also joined them there.

Teru always preferred walking in good-sized groups, where there were many people with whom to converse. She felt that this made for better relations, since, if two people did not get along, each one had several other people they could talk to. Personalities collided less. With only three walkers, tension between two people had a much greater impact, with the third person stuck in the middle. She was happy to take her first steps out of Bombay with a healthy and varied group of seven walkers, representing the U.S., India, and Japan.

However, once on the road, Teru quickly learned that India was unlike any of the places she had traveled in the U.S. and Europe: there were people everywhere, the roads outside the city were often dirt or semi-paved, which meant that dust flew into her face when the wind blew or a car passed, flies swarmed around her when she paused for a break, and the Indian sun felt as if it were right over her shoulder.

As the group made its way across the southern Indian countryside outside Bombay during the first few weeks, conditions became more difficult—the days got hotter and the walkers' bodies became weaker. To avoid the extreme heat, the group walked early in the morning, tried to take a shaded nap in the afternoon, and would walk again in the evening. Even with this routine, the conditions were grueling.

In India, the challenges were unlike what Teru had expected. At other times on the journey, the group had had difficulty finding good food or adequate shelter for the night. In India, however, people regularly offered them food and welcomed them into their homes. Though clean drinking water was not always available, the group traveled with a handheld Swiss water filter that could purify just about any water. The basics, in terms of food and shelter, were largely provided for in India, but the heat and the other conditions were harsh.

It did not take long for one of the walkers, Taz, to get very sick. He was given a diagnosis of typhoid fever and was told to rest. Taz and Star, who prided themselves on living simply, had chosen not to use the water purifier. They figured that it was just an extra and unneeded technological device, and they believed that their systems would eventually adjust to the bacteria in India. Whether this made Taz more susceptible to typhoid fever no one knew, but as a result Taz and Star left the group to rest and recuperate on the beaches of Goa, in western India.

While the walking conditions in India were severe, for Teru the hardest part was not the heat or the flies but the lack of privacy. She said of this part of the journey, "It stretched my abilities to be flexible such that they require a rest before they are tried again." The attention that the group received certainly had its benefits, with plentiful food and housing, but it also became particularly tiring for Teru. Besides during sleep, there was no opportunity for downtime. People were around her non-stop, wanting to get a look at the peace-walking Japanese-American who had just arrived in their town. For Teru, it was as if she were on constant display. Part of her purpose, of course, was to meet local people, but she was surrounded everywhere she went, particularly at night, while staying at the homes of villagers.

In April of 1992, after roughly two months of walking across the dry desert plains of southern and central India, the challenges started to mount. In particular, it was getting hotter, which made the walking harder. Summer had arrived in India, and it would not leave for several months. As a result of the severe heat, both Essrea and Abigail got very sick. They had fevers of 103 degrees and vomited for days, and had barely enough strength to get out of bed. The group concluded that, owing to the conditions and their ill health, it was best to take a train the last couple of hundred kilometers to Delhi.

India had not been all struggle, however. The highlight of the journey for Teru was meeting the tribal people of India, known as the Adivasis, which means "original inhabitants." Representing roughly 8% of the population, the group had once lived in the forests of India, but, as these have been destroyed in order to build cities, they have had to adjust their lifestyle. Teru thought that they were the most physically beautiful people she had ever seen, and their approach to life was simple; they viewed land as communal.

Along the way, the group was also able to network and visit with Gandhi-inspired communities. Most of these had a school for local children, and the inhabitants hand-spun their own cloth for clothes and made money through a number of cottage industries, which according to Teru's notebook included "making soap, incense, clothes, matches, blocks, rope, carpets, or handicrafts." She was inspired by the friendliness and cooperation in these communities.

Resting at the temple in Delhi after the train ride, Teru felt the limits of her physical strength. She did not contemplate quitting, but India had clearly humbled her. It had taught her an important lesson: she could not simply walk anywhere at any time. From here on, the group needed to be more thoughtful about the places they went. Considering that it was now summer in Asia, heeding this lesson meant finding a cooler climate in which to walk.

Years before, when she was at her parents' home in Los Angeles, mapping out a possible route, Teru considered traveling to Pakistan after India. Sitting in the Delhi temple after two months in the grueling Indian heat, Pakistan made more sense than ever. Teru and the other walkers sat down with a map of Pakistan and proceeded to plan a route through the country, the sixth most populous in the world and the second largest with a Muslim majority. Seeking to get as far north as possible, they decided on a route that would start from the capital, Islamabad, and head up the Karakoram Highway, which links Pakistan to China in the north. Since the Karakoram was the highest paved highway in the world, they could think of no better place to walk in the summertime.

I arrived to join the group in Delhi right after they had made their decision. (I had been on the U.S. Walk, too, joining them for the second half of the trek from Oklahoma to New York City.) When asked about the plan, I said that going to Pakistan sounded fine to me, though I knew practically nothing about its history or culture—and I guessed that the same was true for most of the other walkers. None of the group seemed to care. It was cooler in Pakistan, and that was reason enough to go.

I could not quite fathom how the Walk was surviving on the road. I had come with a large backpack full of cans of food, cooking equipment, a sleeping bag, a tent, numerous changes of clothes, several kinds of shoes, and an assortment of books. And my load would have been ten pounds heavier had a small bag not been stolen on a train ride the day before. When I dropped my backpack on the ground, the other walkers looked at me, concerned. In my mind, I had trimmed down as much as I could. One needed to carry certain supplies, I thought. What is the other option—to walk down the road hoping that food and shelter would just appear? Much to my dismay, that was exactly the plan! Though calling anything on the Walk a "plan" was pushing it, since nothing was ever really set.

The other members convinced me to leave everything at the temple except my sleeping bag and a few changes of clothes. "It's just easier to go without," I remember them saying. "Trust us. We have been doing this awhile." Who was I to argue? All I knew was the U.S. Walk, where we had an assortment of support vehicles; I knew practically nothing about walking without such support. I reluctantly put most of my belongings in a separate bag and left it at the temple, hoping that I was not going to starve to death without my cans of food and the cooker. The others' sense of trust, I thought at the time, was either insane or revolutionary. I figured time would give the answer.

As we prepared for the trip to Pakistan, we were without the Japanese monk, who had returned to his temple in Bombay. Mohammad was still with the group and wanted to continue on to Pakistan, but he was having trouble obtaining a passport; once he had that, he could then apply for the necessary visa for Pakistan. While in Delhi, we met with a political official on his behalf, but the situation was complicated by the fact that Mohammad was Muslim and the official was from a nationalist Hindu political party. In the end, his passport application was turned down.

Teru was relieved to have some time to rest at the temple, and was excited about the new plan to go to Pakistan. Though she and I had walked for some months together through the States, I did not know her very well. I knew her as the "Peace Flame woman," and as one of the Walk elders who took care of tasks such as bookkeeping. Like most of my peers, I avoided as many Walk responsibilities as possible, and spent most of my time with my girlfriend at the time, Shanti, and the other twenty-something walkers. There were various Walk subgroups, and Teru's and mine did not come together very often. Still, Teru welcomed me with open arms and treated me as a dear friend from the very first day.

Though India had humbled Teru, she still had excitement and energy for the journey. A new country, she figured, would bring new life to a fairly tired group of walkers. And Pakistan was different in so many ways that the sense of adventure was revived.

After the necessary rest at the temple, Essrea, Teru, Abigail, and I ventured from Delhi, first by train and then by bus, to Islamabad to begin our trek north into China. No one had seen Taz and Star since they left the group to recuperate on the beach in the province of Goa. Teru had mentioned to them that the Walk might head to Pakistan after India, and that they might be able to find the group there. None of us knew when or if the two would locate us, but we had a more important task ahead of us than worrying about their whereabouts—to get the hell out of India and reach the cooler Pakistan, as fast as possible.

Lessons from Walking in Pakistan

Sharing Attention

Since Teru was the oldest and most experienced walker for most of the journey, locals often focused on, and directed their questions, at her. They asked her about the purpose of the Walk, what it hoped to accomplish, and why it was important. Though Teru naturally attracted attention, she never tried to grab it or keep it; instead, she made a concerted effort to share it with others, wanting to give everyone a chance to speak. Teru did not aspire to be an articulate leader who could mesmerize a group with her speaking skills and her presence. This was of little interest to her. Her primary goal was to make sure that every member of the group had the same opportunity.

One day in northern Pakistan, as the group sat under a canopy and enjoyed cold drinks from a nearby store, a young female Pakistani newspaper writer approached the group, seeking to interview Teru and write an article on the Walk for her paper. The woman had heard about the group from a friend, and thought her readers would enjoy learning more about the group's journey through Pakistan. She had a long list of questions.

After Teru answered a number of them, about the purpose and the length of the Walk, she suggested that the woman interview a college-age Malaysian man named Tariq, who had been on the Walk for only about a week. Hearing this, Tariq looked up from massaging his feet, shocked that Teru would ask him to speak about a journey he knew so little about. "You want me to be interviewed?" he asked, surprised. But Teru insisted, responding, "You are a member of this Walk as well, and have your own reasons for joining, and it is important you share what those are. You should be interviewed as well."

It made little difference to Teru that he planned to be with the group for only a few weeks that summer. Even though she had been walking for more than two years, she did not carry any sense of rank or importance. The Walk was not hers. It belonged to everyone who was drawn to it, including the young Malaysian man. Teru was the model of a different type of leader. To her, the strongest group was one in which everyone could speak openly and freely, and no one person drew the focus. She would happily relinquish a group of "followers" to be with a group of "leaders."

Be Like a Child

For Teru, part of surviving and thriving on the Walk was learning to be flexible. Every day, the walkers had no idea what would happen. This was especially true in Asia. Their route could change; the weather might turn from clear and sunny to rainy; the person offering them housing for the night could change his or her mind, leaving them without shelter. The only constant was inconsistency. On most days, Teru woke up knowing very little about things that the average person takes for granted, such as food and shelter. She thus learned to flow with whatever happened. Teru wrote, "When entering a new place, you must be flexible. You must be like a child: curious and fascinated rather than stubborn and habitual."

It was not that she played dumb or did not use her wits; she found that flowing with what was happening was a much easier route than fighting it, that staying open to what the day presented was more fulfilling than trying to make the day turn out as she hoped it would. In fact, it was this flexibility to changing conditions that Teru claimed was essential to surviving on the Walk. When asked in Pakistan what it takes to undertake a journey like this, she answered, "Probably the most important asset is flexibility. Being able to reverse directions if necessary. One moment you are aggressive, the next you can be low-key, even passive, because the situation may change."

One never really knew how a day would unfold, and, for Teru, this accounted for much of the joy and beauty of walking, as it meant she had to be creative and alert; she had to be like a child.

Finding Home

From a young age, Teru often felt as if she did not belong. Growing up as a Japanese-American after World War II, when the memories of Pearl Harbor were still fresh in Americans' minds, she endured her share of suspicion and judgment as she and other Japanese-Americans struggled to integrate back into a culture that was hesitant to trust them again. Though she was often not accepted as an American, she was also not Japanese, since she neither spoke the language nor followed the cultural traditions. The confusion of who she was and where she belonged was enhanced by her internment at Manzanar Camp when she was four years old. In her younger years, the most pressing questions on her mind were "Who am I?" and "Where do I belong?"

As a teenager, Teru hoped that she would gain acceptance in the mainstream population by excelling in school and proving herself. But, even while serving as the class president in high school and excelling academically, the feeling of "otherness" lingered. She later wondered if there was a physical place—a city in the U.S. or a country in Asia—where she might at last feel as if she belonged.

The Walk was, in large part, a way for her to reconcile this feeling of otherness which had plagued her since she was interned as a child. She wrote after completing the journey, "My motivation for doing this walk stems from the experiences of being a minority in the U.S. I wanted out from the racism that I had internalized." Early on, she knew that she had a decision to make: either walk for three and a half years feeling like an outsider everywhere she went or find a sense of home in herself and thus fit in everywhere.

In Pakistan, a little more than halfway through her journey, Teru at last resolved this issue. "Now doing this Walk," she said, sitting down on the grass while taking a break in Pakistan, "I see my home as being right here, wherever I am. I have not been homesick yet." Having discovered this, she said that she could travel in any country and interact with all kinds of people, and this feeling of belonging stayed with her.

While I was on the Walk, I never heard her talk about her home in Los Angeles. She did not utter statements like "When I get home, I'm going to . . . " or "If only I were home, I would . . ." Home was not a far-off place that she hoped to return to someday. L.A. was no more home than a farmer's field in Pakistan. There was little sense of missing something or wishing that she were anywhere else. Likewise, she never spoke about arriving at her final destination, in Hiroshima, as a special event or day. I did not once hear her say, "Once I get to Hiroshima ..." or "I can't wait to get to Hiroshima." She was committed to getting there, but her real destination was wherever she was.

She wrote after the journey, "From the Walk, I learned that no matter where I was, no matter what the people looked like, no matter what language they spoke, that I belonged with them on this planet."

Dealing with Vomit Heads

While 99% of the people were good and generous, there was still that one percent who were not. Teru said that she always had to keep her "intuitive sensor" on to ward off possible danger. A few times in her long journey, she failed to do so. One such time happened on a lonely country road in India. As Teru told it, "I watched a truck pull over and a man get out who seemed to be tending a tire. As I approached, I vaguely sensed ill intention by the way he turned toward me. I was pushing my strolley, and swung wide on the opposite side of the road. He slowly moved forward and put his hand out as if wanting a handshake. I wanted to trust him, but in a split second I knew that my first impression was correct. As I lifted my hand to meet his hand, he groped for my breasts. I screamed in his face. He backed off.

"I was livid, swearing and yelling as I moved away. It reminded me of all the other times men had made physical advances against my wishes. I had such an urge to spit and throw rocks at him, but I knew that was not the answer. I felt such righteous fury. I hope he saw the color red flying out of my mouth along with the splattering of saliva. In this situation, I did not listen completely to my intuition. If I had been more centered, I would have clearly picked up on his intentions and responded appropriately."

Later, when the same thing happened to Abigail in Pakistan, they looked in their small traveler's guidebook for a disparaging word to call such people. The worst they could come up with was translated in English as "vomit head." It was not the best phrase, but it gave them something to use in warding off people with bad intentions.

In the end, Teru claimed, "vomit heads" were a very small minority, and as long as she and the others kept their wits about them they could usually be avoided.

Walk-Time

One of the aspects that was most difficult for new walkers to comprehend was learning to blend with what the group called "walk-time." In walk-time, clocks do not matter. There is nowhere to be at a certain time, no appointments to keep, and no schedule to adhere to. Instead, you follow your own pace and the cycles of nature. In walk-time, the group woke up at sunrise and went to sleep soon after sunset, and much of the day was spent accomplishing the simple task of putting one foot in front of the other. On the Walk, there was usually no one to call or meet. For walkers, there was nowhere else to be except where they were. Life was simple, with little need for watches or planning.

New walkers, however, usually did not adjust easily to this sense of time. In their first few days on the journey, they continually asked questions about when the group would arrive at the next town, what time they would eat lunch, and where they would sleep at night. I did, too, when I joined. The level of the unknown on any given day was more than I had ever experienced.

In Pakistan, one such new member was an English college student named Barnaby, who joined the Walk for a few weeks when he met us while traveling in northern Pakistan. In his first day walking with the group, Barnaby constantly looked at his watch, trying to calculate how long it took to walk the last kilometer, and how many more kilometers the group had to go before arriving at the next town. Every hour or so, he would say, "I estimate it took us forty-five minutes to walk that last kilometer. We must have five more kilometers to go, so that would mean we will arrive in a little less than four hours." This was very odd behavior to experienced members of the group like Teru.

Of course, there were days when the group had to make a decision based on time, such as whether there was enough daylight to walk to the next town where housing would be more likely, but watches were not needed for this. Asking a local could help the group determine the distance to the next town, and a quick look at the sun and the sky let them know how much sunlight was left. Nature was the best guide for such decisions, not a watch.

But, for those accustomed to living on "watch time," this approach was challenging. It was hard for them to grasp that it really made no difference what time their watch read. While this is essential in traditional life, it was completely useless on the Walk. The focus was to be wherever you are. Nothing else was expected.

Teru would not criticize or judge attempts by new walkers to who focused on time. She knew that people were simply trying their best to orient to life on the Walk. She trusted that if they stayed on the journey long enough they would understand the benefits of living without that structure. In response, she would simply direct new walkers' attention to the scenery around them, commenting on a striking cloud, an expansive tree, or a lush valley. By doing this, she would gently invite them to awaken their senses. As this happened, people tended to look at the world around them much more and at their watches much less.

Don't Know

The group often had members who joined for just a short time, often college students and activists, who came with various questions about how one survives on the journey, such as "Where are we going to sleep tonight?" and "What are we going to eat for dinner?" The most common response that Teru would give to the flood of questions by new walkers was "I don't know. It will work out." It took a good deal of trust for new walkers to join the group. They were told to walk in one direction, not knowing how far they would walk that day, when or if they would eat, or where they would sleep. New walkers, however, wanted to think that someone in the group had a plan, and often directed their questions at Teru. But the Walk lived much more in not knowing than in knowing.

This "not knowing" did not arise from not wanting to know, or from a fear of what might happen; instead, it was based on an openness to what might happen, and a trust that basic needs would be provided. For the walkers, not knowing where they were going to sleep on a given night was not a problem; it was an opportunity to keep one's eyes open and possibly meet a new person. Not knowing simply meant that there was space for new learning.

The Walk continued day after day, with the walkers knowing very little. Teru later said, "I never knew from one country to the next how the people would treat us or if we would be able to walk through their country. But I knew that I wanted to believe they would treat us kindly and that we would be able to make it across." Teru tried to pass along this sense of trust and discovery to new walkers. By answering "I don't know" to their questions, she was encouraging a sense of adventure, excitement, and mystery. Rather than "Shit, we really don't know where we will sleep or eat," it was "Cool. We don't know. Let's see what the day brings! How exciting." Not knowing was an opportunity, not a problem.

This was hard for people to understand, but for Teru this was the best and only way for the Walk to survive. It was to live not by trying to know everything at all times but by trusting in the mystery of not knowing.

Since members spent practically all day walking alongside highways, this fearlessness was often referred to as "trusting the road." Walkers would say, "Don't worry, the road will provide food for us. Just trust it." Just who this road was or how it worked could not be explained, but work it did. When I first heard the concept, while walking in Pakistan, I was suspicious. Looking for a pen one day, Ess invited me to "ask the road." I did so, and, sure enough, a dirty but working pen appeared later that day on the side of the road. This made me a convert.

Be Careful Who You Drink With

People have often asked if there were times when Teru, being so vulnerable to people and the elements, feared for her safety. I am not sure of the answer to this, but there was a time in Pakistan when a number of us who were with her were afraid.

A local police chief had offered us a place to stay at his country home. He was a thin man of average height, with a long thick mustache that curled upward at both ends, partially covering his cheeks, giving him a mischievous appearance. At the time, it was me, Teru, Ess, Abigail, and our Pakistani friend, Ashiek. Taz and Star had meet up with the group again in Pakistan, but at this juncture they were on a side trip to visit hot springs.

After about an hour's ride in a jeep, we arrived at the police chief's house. Not long afterward, he brought out several bottles of Jack Daniel's. This was surprising, particularly since I had been told that alcohol was illegal to own or consume in Pakistan. When I asked our host about this, he responded with a chuckle, "For other people, but not for the police. I am the law around here and I do as I please." He then gave me a "leave me the hell alone" stare, and changed the subject.

Our host quickly started to down one glass after another. By the time he had drunk several glasses of whiskey, I began to get seriously concerned. I did not trust him sober, and the more he drank the more outrageous he became, dancing playfully and sitting down close to Essrea and Abigail, much closer than I had ever seen a Pakistani man do. He insisted that Abigail and Ess dance with him, and I could tell as they did that he was getting more turned on by the moment. All the while, he kept his gun close.

He started to exert more influence on us as the evening progressed. Sitting next to Essrea, he asked her a question, but when she turned away from him

107

without answering he grabbed her jaw and forcefully turned her head back toward him, saying, "You are my guest and must speak to me."

I realized that practically no one knew where we were and it would have been no use to call the police if something were to happen. Teru was still enjoying her glass of whiskey, and did not appear burdened by the situation. In fact, she seemed to be enjoying herself: the evening was a far cry from our usual uneventful nights sleeping outside underneath trees or in rural homes after a simple meal. We had not heard music or seen alcohol for some time.

Fortunately, another man showed up later, a banker whom we had met earlier. In the presence of another person, the police chief calmed down. I can't remember ever being so happy to see someone than when the banker walked into the room. I do not know about Teru, but I for one was relieved to have made it through the night without someone getting hurt. The next day, we got a ride back to the main road and went on our way.

Help Those Who Help

Various locals joined us in the countries we traversed, some for only a day, others for months. Our most regular walker in Pakistan, who often served as our guide and translator, was a young man named Ashiek. A non-practicing Muslim, Ashiek dressed more Western than just about anyone else I saw in that part of the world. While we wore loose-fitting airy pants, cotton shirts, and sandals, he walked every day in blue jeans, white tennis shoes, and button-down dress shirts. He had, supposedly, found out about the Walk from a friend of someone whom Teru had met in Europe. Some of us had our suspicions early on that Ashiek was actually a government spy, sent to keep track of our activities.

No one was ever sure, but I suspected that Ashiek may have had other motives. He certainly cared about creating a better world through cross-cultural exchange, but he also asked me a flood of questions about Ess and Abigail. He wanted to know if they had ever been married, what they liked in a man, and how his life might be if someone like him married a Western woman and moved to the U.S. Sadly, or possibly happily, this dream of Ashiek's never came true, at least not from marrying Abigail or Ess.

Ashiek was a good-hearted man who was especially skilled at getting us housing. For the weeks he was with us, we spent many nights sleeping in local homes and eating hot meals. Curious about how he was able to do this, I asked Ashiek one day, "Just what do you tell people about us?" Ashiek grinned slightly. "Oh, that you are very important people from the U.S. on a global mission for peace," he said. "That's it?" I asked, thinking that there might be more, and aware of the smirk on his face. Ashiek smiled and said, "Yeah, that's all."

Ashiek did not know the tradition on the U.S. Walk of taking new names, but shortly after he joined our adventure he told us that he would like to be called something other than his given name. When we asked what it was, he responded proudly, "Stonewall, from the American general Stonewall Jackson. I want to be called Stonewall."

Now, we were a pretty easygoing, live-and-let-live group, but naming oneself after a Confederate general in the American Civil War was pushing our flexibility. Still, we accepted his name, and called him by it when we remembered to do so. I never learned what it was about the name Stonewall that had attracted Ashiek, whether it was just the name or some action that the general performed. However, if I ever needed something from him, all I had to say was "Stonewall, could you come here for a moment?," and Ashiek—all five feet four and 125 pounds of him—would quickly get up and stride proudly and gallantly over to me.

You Can't Walk That Far

Teru was often told by well-meaning locals that she could not walk across their country. On being asked how far it was to a town some distance away, they would say, "It's too far to walk. You must take the bus." Even when Teru or a translator explained that the walkers had traversed thousands of miles on foot and that they could certainly walk to the town in question, still the person would insist that the 100 miles to the town was too far for someone to walk. They just could not fathom how a person could walk such a distance.

Teru came to expect such responses and understood them to be a sign of the self-imposed limits that people place on what they and others can and cannot do. The Walk was, to her, an experiment in questioning and pushing such limitations. "If you don't believe you can do something, you are probably right," she would say—not because it was inherently true but because you believed it to be so. Indeed, had she asked others' advice before embarking on her three-and-a-half-year trek across the globe, they would have likely argued that a fifty-year-old woman walking in foreign countries with no support vehicles or arranged food or housing could not survive for long. Such a feat was outside the realm of what most people thought was possible.

When Teru was told that she could not do something, she often responded, "You may be right, but I am going to try my best." She acknowledged limits but claimed that the best way to find out was to push ahead and try. This, in fact, was a part of the Walk's mission: to show people that more is possible if we trust and believe it. She wrote after the journey, "I have always liked new experiences and risking comfort to stretch my physical, emotional, psychological, social, and political orientations. The Walk was an opportunity to test my abilities and to put my beliefs into action."

So, when she was told that she could not do something, Teru generally did not argue with the person or try to convince them otherwise; she simply showed through her actions a willingness to push the limits of what she and others thought possible. Though there were times when she really could not complete something that she set out to do, by making the effort she always gained in learning and experience. In trying, she would say, there really was no way that she could lose.

Finding the Walkers

Teru usually took a break from the daily act of walking only when every other member wanted to do so—that is, she stopped because otherwise she would have no one to walk with—or when the physical conditions were simply too harsh, such as in Cambodia. However, her twenty-something comrades were more lenient in their use of breaks. This was less true for Essrea and Abigail, but was certainly the case for me and the dynamic simple-living duo of Taz and Star.

Since no one in the group had a cell phone or other communication device, once members left they would not usually know how to find the group a month or two later, after a break. People could send letters, but the group rarely went to a post office to pick them up; and, even when they did receive them and write back, they could not say for certain when they were going to be in a particular city, much less how to locate them once they arrived. Somehow, though, people reconnected.

When I tried to rejoin the group in India, I was sent an address of a Buddhist temple in Delhi that the Walk planned to visit at the end of June. But I had received this address four months before leaving the States, so I knew that it would be a long shot to find them. I arrived in Delhi two weeks before their planned arrival, and thought I might as well try my luck. When I reached the address I was given, the woman at the residence told my taxi driver that the Buddhist monks no longer lived there, and that we could try another temple, about forty-five minutes away. Fortunately, it was there that I found Teru and the others, and just in time, as they had arrived several weeks early, because several walkers had become extremely sick, and were about to leave again in a few days. Had I come when they had planned to be there, I would have missed them completely.

After Taz got sick in India, and he and Star took time off to rest at the beach, the group still had a month or two left before they planned to arrive in Delhi. After Delhi, the group was uncertain about where they would travel next, but they told Star and Taz that they were considering venturing north to Pakistan, where it was cooler. The walkers headed to Pakistan a month later, not sure if or when Taz and Star would try to connect again with them.

While the group was in Islamabad, the capital of Pakistan, Abigail befriended a German juggler named Hilby, and he joined the group for part of the journey. After about a month of walking, Hilby needed to return to Islamabad to extend his visa. While Hilby was with the group, Abigail had given him a Global Walk for a Livable World T-shirt. Hilby was staying at the tourist campground in Islamabad, and happened to be wearing the shirt one day. That same day, Taz and Star just happened to be staying at the campground and walked by him, noticing the shirt.

Hilby was then able to direct Taz and Star to the group's general whereabouts in the north. Had Abigail not befriended Hilby or had he not joined the Walk or had Abigail had not given him the T-shirt or had Hilby not been wearing it that day or had Taz and Star stayed at a different location in Islamabad, the two would have had a very difficult time locating the group.

Still, Taz and Star arrived in Pakistan, a country of more than 100 million people, trusting that somehow they would find their fellow-walkers. They never doubted that they would be guided to them—and, sure enough, they were.

Kashgar, China

Sitting on a bed in a red-and-white room in a government-approved guesthouse in Kashgar, China, Teru sobbed as she hadn't in years. The Walk was coming apart after two successful and incredible years on the road. Everything that she had believed in was now in question. In this northwestern Chinese town, Teru wondered how and if she could continue.

The walkers—Teru, Star, Taz, Ess, Abigail, and I—had just spent three adventuresome months in Pakistan traversing the Karakoram Highway, the highest paved international road in the world, completed in 1986 after twenty arduous years of work. (The steep cliffs made working conditions extremely dangerous, and hundreds of Pakistani and Chinese laborers died.) The road starts near Pakistan's capital, Islamabad, and extends 1,300 kilometers north, to Kashgar. It follows a branch of the ancient trading route known as the Silk Road, of which Kashgar was a hub. It was here that

Alexander the Great, in the fourth century B.C., began his campaign to conquer much of the Indian subcontinent. The path adjacent to the road is believed to be the one followed by Bodhidharma when he brought Buddhism to China. The road is beautiful and dangerous as it cuts between Asia and India—and Teru was thrilled to experience it.

After arriving in Islamabad, the group joined the Karakoram in July of 1992 and set out for China. The first few weeks outside Islamabad were rough, as the group walked along busy highways where the drivers weren't accustomed to obeying street signs or looking out for walkers on the side of the road. But as they made their way north the traffic lessened, the mountains loomed, and the people were much more welcoming. The group walked almost every day, as planned, though they had to hitchhike through the notorious tribal area in Pakistan when a still-frozen glacier prevented them from taking a shortcut in the north. A highlight for many was walking through the legendary Hunza region, from where you can see some of the highest peaks in the world. The group also enjoyed the food, including wild mulberries and apricots, as well as sourdough pancakes.

Teru loved the journey in northern Pakistan—rugged, friendly people, staggering views, children who would run up and offer to help push her strolley, and often good sleeping options at night, both indoors, at family homes, and outside, in lush fields. The climate in the higher elevations of Pakistan was also a relief from the extreme heat that Teru had experienced while walking from Bombay to Delhi. Though the steep terrain presented physical challenges for her in walking with the strolley, Teru's spirits were high and most days she had no trouble keeping up with the rest of the group.

When the walkers arrived in Sust, the last town on the Karakoram before

China, they already knew that they wouldn't be able to walk in China. Just to reach China from Pakistan on the Karakoram Highway, one would have to travel over the Khunjerab Pass, which, at an elevation of more than 15,000 feet, is the highest paved border crossing in the world. Then, there are numerous sections in China that are off limits to foreigners for military reasons. Furthermore, at the time, travelers could stay only at approved government-sanctioned guesthouses, which are difficult to find while walking in the countryside. Though the group could not walk in China, they still wanted to visit it and see the end of the Karakoram Highway, even if it had to be by bus. Teru, however, had no idea of the emotional challenges that her short stay in China would bring.

The tears that Teru shed at the guesthouse were caused by a number of events. First, many of her fellow-walkers had left her, either for family reasons or because they needed time off. Taz and Star had departed in Kashgar to hitchhike across China, and planned to fly back to the States from Shanghai, unsure if they would return again. Abigail had returned home for a few months to attend her sister's wedding, and planned to rendezvous with the group again back in Delhi. I had been with the group in Pakistan, and left Kashgar a few days before to work on a book back in the States. The group was thinning out fast. This left just Teru and Ess— and Ess had recently told Teru that she needed a few months off from "walk life" and the grueling task of carrying all her belongings day after day. Ess wanted to travel by herself. This meant that Teru was essentially alone until she, Abigail, and Ess regrouped a few months later in Delhi. And even then they weren't sure what route they would take.

However, this was only partly the cause of Teru's tears. Another companion had also left her in Kashgar. The Hiroshima Peace Flame, which she had carried and nurtured every day for the previous two years, had shown to hundreds if not thousands of people, and had slept next to each night, had gone out. She was devastated.

It happened because she had been given the wrong kind of fuel at a local shop. Though the flame stayed lit for a short time after she filled the lantern, on returning to her room at the guesthouse her mouth opened and her eyes watered on seeing that her most dependable companion was gone. For two years she had watched the flame glowing in her lantern. It represented the purpose and meaning of the journey, both the pain left by war and the hope for a better world. It was as if her best friend and the entire purpose of the Walk had been taken from her.

The flame had gone out once before, just after the walkers crossed from Belgium into the Netherlands. If the flame went out, it needed to be relit by an offshoot of the Hiroshima Peace Flame. Fortunately, a friend in the Netherlands offered to go to Dover, England, to get such an offshoot from a supporter who, when Teru visited him, had put the flame on the pilot light of his gas stove. For Teru, this meant that the pilot light was now the Peace Flame. But there was no such person in China or Pakistan, and she was unaware of any site or temple in surrounding countries that housed the flame.

Many people have asked why she did not simply light a match to create a new flame and call it a Peace Flame. After all, it is just a flame, and she would be the only one who knew that it was not the Hiroshima Peace Flame. Why did it matter to her? Teru's decision not to relight the flame tells us a great deal about her. It was not just a flame to her; it represented the story she wanted to tell, and the history she sought to pass on. It had a spirit and a meaning that could not be re-created. For better or worse, this is how she viewed it.

Her only other option, then, was to see if she could retrieve an offshoot of the flame as she had done in Europe. However, the only places besides Europe that housed it were in the U.S. and Japan. While she was not willing to light a new flame, the time, effort, and resources it would take to fly to Japan or Europe to get a new offshoot of the flame were significant and seemed to go against the spirit of the Walk.

Then Teru remembered, "Abigail is in New York and returning in a month, and there is a place with the flame there." She called Abigail on the phone, still emotionally distraught, and asked her to stop in New York City at the Cathedral of St. John the Divine and try to bring the flame back with her to Asia. She explained to Abigail how she carried it on planes by using a handwarmer and going to the bathroom to light new pieces of charcoal every four hours.

Abigail agreed, but her mother, wanting to make sure it was safe and not understanding that it was against airline rules, called the airlines to inquire about how Abigail could bring the flame on the flight. As a result, Abigail's ticket was flagged, and, when she arrived at the airport with the flame in the handwarmer, officials pulled her aside and refused to allow her to bring it on the flight. Ab broke down in tears, knowing how much the flame meant to Teru, and pleaded with the officials, but without success.

It is hard to describe what the flame meant to Teru. She said of it, "Keeping the flame lit took enormous effort and care; the kind of care one gives to a young child who always has to be looked after." With her "child" gone, a shrinking number of walkers, and extremely harsh conditions for walking, Teru was not sure how or if they would be able to cross Southeast Asia and make it to Japan.

Most of the group was unaware of Teru's hardship at the time. She generally did not tell people about her own worries and needs. Before the journey, she had resolved to be a counselor and a support to the other walkers, and never to complain or to discuss problems she was having, unless it was in a co-counseling session. This meant that Teru often kept her needs hidden. Many of us at the time assumed that she, as the elder and guiding force of the Walk, could handle anything. It was only years after the Walk that I better understood the sense of abandonment she felt in Kashgar as all her twenty-something walkers were "doing their own thing," unable to see Teru's needs, which she was not comfortable expressing.

In many ways, one of Teru's great strengths was that she completely accepted people as they were and trusted them to follow their own path. At times, however, this ability could also be a weakness, for, in this case, Teru did not let anyone know that she wanted them to stay. If she had told me that she would love for me to stay on the journey until other walkers could join her, I would have been happy to do so. But I learned only years later that she wanted this. Because she was such a strong, steady force on the Walk, many of us assumed that she could always take care of herself.

All these factors forced Teru to question her purpose on the Walk. It was no longer about the Peace Flame, since the flame was no longer with her. It was not about community, since everyone else was gone. It was also not about walking every step as planned, since she and the others had already had to change their route and take other means of travel several times.

Why am I walking? she asked herself, in a moment of desperation and inner turmoil. The flame had meant so much to her, more than most of the other walkers could understand at the time. Then Teru remembered what it represented to her: the possibility for peace, and a world where children would not have to suffer the repercussions of war, through either internment or the loss of a family member. The flame would now need to live inside her.

After traveling by herself for four to six weeks in Pakistan, Teru met up with Abigail and Essrea in Delhi to continue the journey.

Lessons from Walking in Nepal, Thailand, and Cambodia
Adjusting

In this part of the journey, Teru learned the value of adjusting. The terrain and the walking conditions in Asia were much more difficult than she had expected, and more difficult than she had experienced anywhere else. There was intense heat, countless bugs, all kinds of diseases, and often inaccurate maps, all of which made walking challenging and at times utterly frustrating. As a result, the group had to continually adjust their route and their expectations. Not doing so could have put the walkers' lives at risk, and would have done little to help their cause. Though she had wanted to walk every step across countries like India and Nepal, once she was in Asia she realized that it would not be possible under the current conditions.

But this was not the only adjustment. Teru also had to adjust to living and walking without the flame. She had always thought that the flame would be with her, and that she would proudly and enthusiastically return it to its home at Peace Park in Hiroshima. She never imagined herself walking without the flame, yet that was the situation in which she found herself. She had to adjust to not having a flame to tend, to remind her of her mission, to sleep next to at night, and to help initiate conversations with people she met. She was a different kind of walker now. Without the flame, she had to find other ways of reminding herself of her mission and of engaging locals on issues of peace and sustainability.

A third adjustment was to the over-all atmosphere of the group. There was not the excitement and enthusiasm of the early years. After roughly two and a half years on the road, people were tired. There were more blisters, sore legs, and hurting backs. People were still able to walk, but there was not the usual bounce in their stride. Life on the road, while exciting, was also grueling, and over time it took a toll.

Teru had to adjust to all this. She knew that in this phase it was, in many ways, a new Walk. In her final year of walking, she realized that, in order to make the most of the journey, she had to constantly adjust to address the conditions that presented themselves.

Take Advice Lightly

Teru also learned on the Walk to take the usually well-meaning advice she received very lightly. Locals often gave her information that in the end proved incorrect. They said, for example, that the next town was a certain number of kilometers away, when it turned out to be much farther, or that there was no food for five kilometers, when in fact there was a store ten minutes down the road. While most people meant well, Teru learned not to completely trust or abide by all the information she received. At times, she received different answers to the same question: someone said it was five kilometers to the next town, and someone else said it was ten. Since there was often no way of knowing the right answer, she had to trust her own instincts and experience.

Sometimes the information she received was not only different but contrary. This was the case when she and the others crossed the border from Hungary into Yugoslavia. It was early evening when the walkers took their first steps in the country, and they looked for a place to sleep outdoors, near the border. They saw few houses nearby and the next town was some distance away. They noticed a lush, grassy field with trees surrounding it and thought it might be an ideal place to sleep that night. Uncertain who owned the land, they asked two men standing nearby if they could camp in the field that night. One of the men said no, claiming that the field was off limits and there was definitely no camping allowed. The other man said that it would be fine to camp there, arguing that it was just a field, and no one would care. With two differing opinions, they had to trust their instincts, which were likely influenced by their fatigue. In the end, they decided to take the second person's advice, and went on to have a wonderful night's sleep in the verdant field. The next morning, as an added surprise, they awoke to a man approaching them with freshly brewed coffee for each walker. It was their first experience of Yugoslavian generosity, and a sign that the group had made the right decision after all.

Teru learned on this and many other occasions that, while people mean well and generally offer the best information they can, all of it had to be taken lightly, and in the end she had to trust her own instincts.

The Power of Women

Teru thought it was fascinating that throughout the journey women were the core of the Walk. In the U.S. segment, women were the most active organizers and took the most responsibility. In Western Europe, the group consisted primarily of three women (Teru, Carolyn Latierra, and Birgit Mertens); the three of them walked the first four and a half months through Europe, supporting and helping one another along the way.

In Eastern Europe, the group took on its first male Phase II member, Taz. He joined in Budapest, but the gender imbalance on the Walk remained, as he was accompanied by three women: Star, Essrea, and Abigail. For most of the Walk through Eastern Europe, the group consisted of six women and one or two men. While two men later joined them on the Bombay-to-Delhi segment, in India, and I accompanied the group in Pakistan and Japan, there was never a time in Europe, Asia, or Japan when men outnumbered women. The Walk was clearly a women-inspired journey.

For Teru, this was just one example of the power of the feminine. It was a myth, she said, that men were stronger than women. Men might be able to lift heavier weights or punch harder, but they were often not as strong as women over long distances. For efforts that took steady commitment over many years, women were usually more suitable. The Walk was not a power lift; it was a test in gentle but steady endurance and flexibility.

While Teru appreciated both the masculine and the feminine, the state of the planet revealed a culture in which the masculine energy was out of balance and the feminine was desperately needed. In fact, qualities often associated with the feminine, such as the ability to blend and compromise, were the same essential ingredients needed to walk for so many years on the road.

Possibly owing to the high proportion of women on the journey, women were also the main supporters of the group over the three years. Women, often mothers and grandmothers, were usually the ones to provide the walkers with food, shelter, and other needs. They were the most apt to interact with the group

and offer their help. Teru learned from the journey the power of and need for feminine energy, and that the qualities most associated with the feminine were also the ones most needed to create a more livable world.

Teru wrote of the women on the Walk, "A questioning mind and a bit of irreverence for authority may get one in trouble, but these qualities definitely contribute to the integrity of any forward-moving group. All of us women had acquired these essential attitudes during our formative years and this helped us immensely on the Walk."

A Global Citizen

Teru may have started the Walk as a Japanese-American, but she ended it as something she liked to call "A Global Mutt." Each country had an impact on her, and expanded her understanding of herself and the world. The people, the clothes, the mannerisms, the style of dress, the ways of speaking—in each country she was influenced by her interactions and experiences. She wrote, "I picked up parts of every culture that I have walked through. Each country expanded my beliefs and customs even more. As a Japanese-American, I realized that I did not need to try to be just one thing, but that I could be myself, which is a mix not only of American and Japanese but of every culture I have been through and experience I have had."

While walking through each country, she did not want to keep a safe and comfortable distance from the locals, and be unwilling to be affected by her surroundings. Instead, she dove into each culture, and tried to learn as much as she could about the beliefs and traditions. She wanted to put herself in the locals' shoes, to see life from their eyes, whether it was a European farmer or a Japanese businessman. Teru expressed it this way: "In each country, I tried to wear their style of clothes, eat their foods (though not always with the customary utensils), participate in their religious practices, and see the world from their perspective. In doing so, I was touched and impressed by people everywhere I went."

While her American and Japanese traits were still very strong components in her, Teru carried with her many qualities of the people that she had come across: she learned simplicity from the East Germans, generosity from the Dutch, courage from the Polish, and the importance of community from Indians. Teru absorbed these qualities, so that her own approach to the world began to shift. Over time, she started to feel less like a Japanese-American and more like a global citizen.

Even though her parents were full-blooded Japanese and she was raised in the U.S., the Walk helped open Teru up to other qualities. She would say at times, "Why not be impacted by the people and places you come across? It shows you that you are not just one thing. No one is just an American or just Japanese. We are all connected. Walking across the world helped remind me of this." She claimed, however, that a person need not walk across the world to learn this, that each day we are given opportunities to learn from the world around us. If we pay attention and are willing to be affected, the world will continually teach us and show us that we are more than we think we are.

Letting Go

Teru was initially inspired, in part, by the pain she felt as a young child interned by her own country during World War II. This experience set the stage for much of her life. Over time, however, Teru realized that this "story of her life" also had limitations. She saw that she could not live her highest beliefs while still identifying as "someone who had been hurt by her own country." She had carried this pain with her, looking for other opportunities where she might also be rejected. On the Walk, Teru realized how much this story repeated itself, how often she looked for rejection, and she vowed not to repeat it. She wrote, "Imagine going across the globe looking for rejection! I had to let those feelings go."

This "old story" and the hurt around it became less interesting over time. She wrote, "Living by one's highest beliefs requires climbing out of old habits, patterns, stories, and fears. My old story from being incarcerated in Manzanar camp was feeling that I didn't belong, always looking for signs of rejection. I could not function optimally when acting on those old feelings of rejection and fear." Essentially, she had to let go of "her story," as powerful and compelling as it was.

It was her story that had in part motivated her to embark on such a grueling journey, and yet in the end it was also her story that was preventing her from living fully. She could no longer carry the hurt from that event and still live with an open heart. The story of how her country had wronged her, how it had killed so many innocent Japanese civilians, and how it had changed the world through its use of the atomic bomb, how she and others had been hurt . . . the facts were true, but the old pain that she still carried from it was holding her back. She wanted to be free of that pain, and at the same time still act on her highest beliefs and convictions.

For Teru, this meant setting a new pattern, different from the one she had been living. Instead of believing the "story of rejection," she decided to stop feeding it. For her, this meant "deciding to include myself everywhere and to stand up for what I wanted no matter how scared or embarrassed I felt." She also made fewer distinctions between the good people and the bad people. In the old story, the U.S. was the evildoer, but she knew that Japan, too, had committed atrocities in World War II, and other countries would likely have used nuclear weapons in the conflict had they developed the means to do so.

At one point in the journey while in Asia, the decision became blatantly clear. She said of that time, "I knew I was faced with a choice: stay confused at the crossroads holding on to those old feelings, or make an effort to change and no longer live with the fear of rejection." The hurt she felt, Teru realized, had served its purpose: it had developed her into a powerful peace activist, yet, in order to be the openhearted, compassionate activist that she knew was inside her, she had to let this hurt go. She had to let go of her story, and instead open herself up to a bigger world, where the possibilities were vast.

Welcome Differences

All the walkers had their own reasons for walking. Teru loved that such diversity existed, and viewed such differences as strengths that should be welcomed. She wrote, "If we look at our differences as oppositions, we only further create separation. If we look at them with curiosity and interest, we make the space for understanding and appreciation."

For Teru, this was very much the heart of her Walk: to deepen understanding through direct contact and knowledge of both our strengths and our differences. This meant learning both how to speak up and how to listen. When contrary views were present, instead of presenting her idea as the absolute truth she tried to express herself in a way that encouraged dialogue. When there was a difference of opinion in the group about a direction or a route to take, rather than saying, "We should do this," she would approach the discussion with "This is how I see the situation, and this is what I think about it. What do others think?"

For Teru, it was important in any dialogue to see that no one owned the truth, no one person's views were necessarily better than anyone else's. Such a view only led to discord and war. However, she believed that by speaking and appreciating differences a greater sense of community could be discovered. In this sense, Teru sought to understand more than to convince, to build community more than to find which person in the group was "right."

Phnom Penh, Cambodia

"How the hell do I keep going?" Teru said to herself, after about a week of walking in the dry, flat Cambodian countryside. It was excruciatingly hot, flies swarmed around her, she was exhausted, and she had not had a hearty meal in more than a week. There was no clean drinking water nearby (the group no longer carried a water filter), and anytime she stepped off the road she had to worry about setting off one of the many land mines still buried in the fields.

Along with this, her back ached from the weight of her backpack. (She had retired her strolley in India, since she no longer needed to transport the extra supplies for the flame.) Carrying a pack, even a light one, proved to be difficult, and she was struggling to keep up with the other walkers, all of whom were more than twenty years her junior. In good conditions, carrying a small backpack was fine, but in the challenging terrain and climate of Cambodia it felt as if it weighed a hundred pounds. Now, after more than two years of walking, she was beginning to tire.

"I must keep going," Teru told herself, swatting away flies and trying to get energy into her legs, though she had little strength left. "You can do it." The group, including Taz, Essrea, Abigail, and Abigail's boyfriend, Hilby, had crossed the Thai-Cambodian border a week earlier. They were en route to Angkor Wat, the famous twelfth-century temple that was built to honor the Hindu god Vishnu. From there, they planned to walk to the capital of Cambodia, Phnom Penh, then on to Vietnam. But Teru was unsure whether she could make it any farther. In her effort to be the "strong supportive elder," she was hesitant to share her struggles with the rest of the group. "I just have to keep going," she repeated, focusing her attention on her legs.

The months since leaving Kashgar, China, after losing the flame, had been fairly pleasant. After regrouping with Ab and Ess in Delhi, and walking a little more in India, the three followed their plan to trek in as many Asian countries as possible. After India, they walked for several weeks through the friendly mountainous nation of Nepal. Then they returned to India and flew to Bangkok, since they could not get permission to walk through the military-controlled state of Burma to get to Thailand.

Much like India, Cambodia presented Teru with extreme challenges—the flies, the heat, little access to clean water, and the extra issue of land mines. At the time, there were somewhere between five and ten million land mines left over from the two-decade-long war that had ravaged the country. With a population of roughly eleven million, there was about one land mine for every one or two people. The effort to dismantle them was already under way, but one never knew where a land mine might be. This added to the tension and unease that plagued Teru.

One day, Ess could tell that Teru was struggling. "Do you think it might help to talk?" Ess asked, offering to listen and aid Teru in processing the emotions she was feeling. "Sure," Teru said, "I would be happy to listen to you." Always the helper, Teru thought that Ess was asking Teru for her support. "No," Ess explained, "I am offering to support you. You look like you are having a hard time. Do you want to talk about it?" Teru smiled in gratitude, happy to realize that Ess had noticed. "Yes, of course."

Teru proceeded to share with Ess the challenges she faced, and the pressure she felt to keep going, to walk as much of the way to Hiroshima as possible. With Ess listening and offering support, Teru realized that she, like everyone else, needed breaks at times, and that it would help no one for her to become seriously ill trying to walk every step across Cambodia. Though she had hoped that her difficulty would pass, each day for the previous week she had awakened feeling worse than the day before. As a result of their conversation, Teru considered taking a bus ahead to Phnom Penh and wait for the others there.

This was not an easy decision for Teru, because she felt that, as a Global Walker, she should be walking every day, not resting. Yet the challenges of the Walk lifestyle were significant: consistently walking fifteen miles day after day; living outside in ever-changing weather conditions, from rain to snow to heat; sleeping every night in a new place, often with little padding underneath her; and eating whatever food one happened to come across, sometimes spicy, other times bland, and not always agreeable to the stomach. While such a life was exciting and exhilarating, it also included days of struggle, and, in Cambodia more than anywhere else, Teru felt this. She decided to take the bus to Phnom Penh.

At a guesthouse in Cambodia, Teru lay on a thin bed and reflected on her more than two years of walking. Now, about three-quarters of the way to her destination, she could sense the end in sight: Hiroshima, Japan. She would finish the Walk in the country of her ancestors, and in the city that more than anywhere in the world has experienced the devastation of nuclear weapons. For the first time since taking that initial step near the Pacific Ocean in California, she could feel the finish approaching. Japan was not that far away.

As she reflected on her journey, she realized how much Asia had humbled her; she no longer believed that she could walk no matter the terrain or the climate. Now, looking back from a guesthouse in Phnom Penh, the U.S. and European segments seemed easy: there had been no land mines to avoid, no regular 110-degree heat to manage, no malaria and other diseases to fend off, and little problem finding plenty of edible food and clean drinking water.

However, Asia had its own lessons to teach. While Teru was at times frustrated by the challenging conditions, she could now see that they had a purpose. The Walk is progressing much as it should, she determined. There were lessons in not having the strength to keep walking across Cambodia, since it refocused her on her mission: to engage people on issues of peace and sustainability. This was, in large part, why she was walking. It was never an endurance test. If Asia had been easier and she were able to walk every step, she could have easily forgotten her mission. Had she been able to do that and failed to connect with the people along the way, she would have arrived in Hiroshima feeling a void, a vague sense that though she had walked many steps, she had not done much for peace.

On that thin mattress in the Phnom Penh guesthouse, Teru understood that this was simply one phase of the journey. It was the third year of the Walk—of course it did not have the vigor and hope of the early years; of course she and the others were tiring. And yet each phase, from the zest of the early years to the fatigue of the later, had a purpose. And the teaching in Asia was that she understand her physical limits and remember that she was much more than just a walker.

A few weeks later, the other walkers arrived in the capital, and the group explored their options. The plan after Cambodia was to walk for a few months in Vietnam, then make their way to Japan for the final three-month trek from Tokyo to Hiroshima, which they planned to do with a group of Japanese Buddhist monks. However, on speaking with a number of travelers who had recently come from Vietnam, they learned that the country had, only three weeks earlier, lifted travel restrictions for foreigners. Before that time, as in China, foreigners could stay only in pre-approved guesthouses. Though the change in the law gave the group more possibilities, the travelers informed them that most people outside the cities were not aware of the rule change. And even those who had heard of the change did not trust it, and would not likely risk punishment by letting the group of peace walkers stay in their homes or sleep in their fields.

With this information, the group ventured from Cambodia to Vietnam, uncertain of how they would be treated and how much they would be able to walk in this ancient country.

Lessons from Walking in Vietnam and Japan
Do What You Can

Probably the biggest lesson that Teru learned in this phase of the journey was to "do what you can." She was a Global Walker, and wanted to be walking just about every day. But it was not that simple, owing, in part, to her energy level, the walking conditions, or sometimes the customs and laws of a country. In Vietnam, it turned out that, as a result of the old Communist laws that forbade people to take in travelers, it was a very challenging country in which to walk. Teru and the others, therefore, spent their time more as tourists than as walkers. This was hard for Teru, yet it provided her with an opportunity to put the lesson she had learned in Phnom Penh into action. It gave her a chance to live her teachings, either while walking or not.

Teru had always had a strong sense of commitment. In fact, it was her determination and strong character that led her to embark on the journey in the first place. Without these qualities, she would have stayed at home, and been one more person who complained about the world without taking action. It was her commitment to issues of peace and sustainability that had inspired her to spend the previous few years on the road. However, in this phase of the journey, the lesson that she learned was not about determination but about surrender. Life was inviting her to let go instead of continue to push forward.

Teru noticed how sometimes she judged herself for "not doing more," even though she had spent the previous several years on the road trying to promote peace and sustainability. "If you are not walking every step of the way or every day," her mind would say, "you are not doing anything." This was the old conditioning, stemming in part from Teru's Japanese upbringing, which emphasized commitment and striving no matter the conditions. Teru valued this part of her, but it was not what was needed in this phase of the journey.

When she could surrender, and simply do what she could do, she found that she could promote peace no matter the situation.

Not Lacking

Teru took quite seriously the impact she had on the world. The Walk was, in part, a way to live her highest beliefs. To do this, she had not only to talk about peace and sustainability but to express this in her life, to make her actions say as much as her words. This involved paying particular attention to how she affected the places that she visited. She wrote, "Entering a space, you inevitably affect that place. On the Walk, I entered areas where they had never seen an American. So I knew their vision of our country would lie greatly in their experiences with me."

This was a great responsibility. Teru knew that, in the past, groups entering new countries had done so oppressively—to convert the country to their religion, or to convince its people that they were primitive and needed to be modernized. Too often, the more powerful group used its power to control the less powerful one. This was a pattern that Teru resolved not to repeat. She did not want to suggest that "America's ways" were inherently better than those of the countries in which she traveled. This was particularly true in economically poor countries such as Cambodia and Vietnam. She did not want to make the locals feel as if they needed to be different than what they were.

While on the Walk, Teru became concerned about multinational companies and media conglomerates trying to bring American movies to less developed countries and to sell the American lifestyle. Though she loved America and would never live anywhere else, she was suspicious about any country's effort to overpower the beliefs of another. America's ways were great for Americans, she thought, but that did not mean that they were right for other countries. She wrote, "People are subjected to American symbols that often do not reflect their own vision. We attempt to make our ideals, their ideals."

Teru did not want to follow this pattern. She had an important responsibility, which she expressed this way: "As travelers from wealthy countries, we can too easily push our country's ways onto the place we visit, subtly giving the locals the feeling that they are behind the times and must change to be more progressive, more advanced. We give them the idea that to be simple is to be ignorant."

Teru worked hard to do just the opposite, to make people feel at ease, whether she was staying in a million-dollar home in Greece or a mud hut in Pakistan. She did this by complimenting people's cultures and traditions, and showing an interest in their lifestyle. She wanted people to feel that their lives were full, not lacking. She sought to inspire them, not to follow America's or anyone else's definition of success but to find and live their own.

That Is Not How We Do Things

In every country, a big challenge for the group was adjusting to the ways and traditions of the local culture. People spoke different languages, held various beliefs, and followed an assortment of practices and religions. There was little time or even interest among the walkers to learn the cultural habits of a country before they entered it. Since they rarely carried or read guidebooks, they often stepped into a country unaware of the norms. Thus, the only way for Teru and the others to learn what was accepted and what was not was to pay attention. They did this by acting naturally and noticing when someone looked shocked or upset; from people's responses, they could determine if they had just broken an unspoken rule of a culture. As Teru once said, "People do not always tell you what their norms are, as they are so used to them. They do not even think of it as a cultural norm. Sometimes the only way we knew that a rule existed was after we broke it."

These differences in culture included everything from dress to eating. In Europe, people often ate with a fork; in Thailand, a spoon was common; in the Indian countryside, people often ate with their hands; and in Japan chopsticks were the norm. What was accepted and expected changed from one culture to the next, at times drastically. This was just as true with mannerisms and other behavior. An action that was received warmly in one culture could be completely unacceptable in another.

In Europe, for example, it was accepted for women to wear shorts and T-shirts on hot days; no one would treat them any differently in such attire. In Pakistan, however, this was completely unacceptable. In that culture, women should at the minimum wear long sleeves and have a shawl or other garment covering the head. A woman walking down the street wearing a short-sleeved T-shirt, a Pakistani man explained to the group, was akin to a woman walking naked down the street in the U.S. Little did Teru and the others know on entering Pakistan just how serious the Pakistanis were about how women should dress.

The greatest challenge in this regard, however, was likely in Japan. Teru never knew just how American she had become until she arrived in Japan. For the first ten days, Teru and the others (Essrea, Taz, Abigail, Hilby, and I) walked with a group of Japanese monks and their supporters. The monks had conducted a walk from Tokyo to Hiroshima every year in memory of the bombing, ending on August 6th, Hiroshima Day. Teru had great respect for the monks, who had let her stay at their temples throughout her journey.

Although the six of us non-Japanese and the fifteen or so Japanese members shared an interest in peace-walking, we soon found that we had vastly different accepted norms of behavior. One example of this was revealed on daily tasks. While we were with the Japanese group, we often slept in temples and at supporters' homes, and on waking in the morning the non-Japanese members generally folded up their  futons and put them away, and then, if there was time, they relaxed or wrote in their journals, trusting that each person would take care of his or her own things. The Japanese members, however, felt that a task was not completed until everyone was done, so after putting away their futons they would help others. They thought of themselves as members of a group first, and as individuals second.

Other conflicts arose that reflected the "individual thinking" of the non-Japanese and the "group thinking" of the Japanese. Sadly, there was no one present who spoke fluent Japanese and English, so communication was very difficult—and no doubt much was lost in the attempts at translation. The misunderstandings became so destabilizing that the two groups decided to split up and peace-walk separately from Tokyo to Hiroshima.

Teru was disappointed that it turned out this way, but it was also freeing to be on her own with her comrades again. The time with the monks provided an important lesson in the need for dialogue, and the difficulty of living together without a common language in which to discuss issues that come up. She learned how conflict can arise not only out of fundamental differences in core beliefs but out of varying views of "accepted" and "unaccepted" modes of behavior.

Clarifying Priorities

Teru was fortunate in midlife to have achieved something of the American Dream, living what she called a "nice, comfortable middle-class life." She and her husband had all the material trappings of happiness: a large, suburban, two-story house with four bedrooms, a formal dining room, coordinated furniture, carpets, and drapes, a swimming pool, and two cars. She lived in a lovely neighborhood, had an active social life, and was "queen of the household." Her priorities during this time were to keep her house clean, to dress nicely, and to host good parties. Teru enjoyed this lifestyle for a time, but as the years passed it became too limiting. She felt as if she were standing on a pedestal and could fall off at any moment.

She later got involved in peace issues, organized events at her house to promote better race relations, and was active in calling for fair-housing laws. The Walk was an extension of this transformation in which she asked, "What are my priorities? If I lived my life by my deepest values, how would I do so?"

The Walk gave her a chance to discover and live her priorities to an even more fulfilling degree. For Teru, it was an opportunity to align her actions with her beliefs more completely. She wrote, "There is something about walking through a country that makes your priorities become very clear. When you focus on the basics—food, shelter, water, friendship—you become a part of the land, in tune with the rhythm of a country."

It was this attunement to the land and to people that Teru experienced through walking. She focused her attention less on how she looked and more on how she lived. Her priorities were not the latest furniture or clothes but the basics of living. She wrote, "When you have to carry all your possessions with you, the game becomes trying to get less, not striving for more. When you know you have to carry it with you, your priorities get very clear."

These priorities increasingly focused on living simply and giving her full attention to those she met, whether it was a fellow-walker with whom she lived every day or a local farmer whom she would likely never see again. The Walk taught her that, at the end of the day, it didn't matter how far she had walked or how many people she had met; what mattered was how she had lived her life, particularly in her interactions with others.

Avoiding Accidents

During the three and a half years walking, the group suffered no major accidents. No one was hit by a car, hurt by an angry local, or injured in a fall. There were, of course, some scrapes and bruises, and an occasional twisted ankle, but nothing serious. This was amazing to Teru, since for most of the journey the group walked alongside roads where cars traveling fifty to sixty miles an hour sped by within a few yards of them. Any number of events could have easily injured a walker quite severely.

When Teru was asked why this was the case, she responded, "I think part of it was due to our high expectations. We always acted as if everything would work out fine and we thought positively about the cultures we visited." For Teru, avoiding accidents had much to do with the group's focusing on the positive instead of the negative: "We expected to meet extraordinary people to help us, and we were always on the lookout for them."

She also believed that much of the good fortune they received was because they were walking for a cause. While the Walk was entertaining at times, and was a test of their physical abilities, neither of these was the main purpose. As Teru explained it, "we were walking not just for ourselves but for the greater good: world peace. With such a focus, you make yourself more available for kindness and magic."

While there was no way to guarantee that an inattentive driver would not swerve to the side of the road and injure them, or that an irresponsible teenager would not drive by and throw a beer bottle at them, Teru chose not to focus on such possibilities. She couldn't entertain such scenarios and still walk every day. Instead of thinking about the negative events that might happen, Teru put her attention on the incredible people and other positive events they could encounter on any given day. She was on the lookout for the good and believed that amazing experiences would occur if only she kept her mind and heart open to them.

In fact, she thought that this attentiveness was another factor that helped the group stay safe. Lingering in the past or getting emotionally caught up in events causes people to make mistakes. She wrote, "When you dwell on the past, accidents and poor judgments are more likely. When we let our fears and distresses take us over, accidents are usually close by."

Speaking Out

It could have been her internment when she was young, or possibly her efforts to stop the war in Vietnam, but somewhere along the way Teru learned the importance of raising her voice and speaking out. This was true on the U.S. segment, when one of the walkers, a Native American man, had an alcohol problem and kept returning to the community drunk. In a meeting, Teru confronted him with directness and compassion, making it clear that while she and the others loved him, he had to get help for his addiction.

Another time, when a member made allegations against Joan Bokaer, the Walk visionary, it was Teru who most vigorously spoke up in her defense. Teru did not raise her voice often, but, when she did, it was loud and clear. She did not care what people thought of her, or believe that it wasn't ladylike for a woman to yell or be forceful.

Sometimes this need to speak up surfaced in other areas. When an official approached her in Cairo and tried to fine her for spitting sunflower-seed shells on the floor of a subway, Teru refused to cooperate. The official demanded that she pay a fine equivalent to $15 U.S. dollars. Teru claimed that the fine was unfair, since there were no posted signs saying that such an action was wrong. At this, the official became irate, threatening to call the police and have her arrested if she did not pay the fine. Teru smiled at the thought of them dragging her, a woman on a global peace walk, off to jail for spitting sunflower seeds on the floor of a subway. Seeing Teru smile only made the official angrier. But Teru just said to the official, "Go ahead. Call the police. I'll wait." At this, the official backed down and Teru went on her way.

Another time, when I was with Teru in Pakistan, we noticed two young men fighting. We had no idea of the cause, since neither of us could understand the language. However, the men were screaming at each other at the top of their lungs, and occasionally exchanging shoves. Before I knew it, Teru was standing between the two, screaming at both of them just as loudly as they were. "What's your problem?" she yelled. "Stop it!" Neither of the men knew quite how to respond to this middle-aged Japanese-American woman who put herself right in the center of their fight. But she got her point across and eventually the men went their separate ways.

Peace Park, Hiroshima, Japan

On August 6, 1993, a sunny, cloudless day, Teru stood with her friend Kaz, an atomic-bomb survivor, in Hiroshima's Peace Park, which commemorates the dropping of the atomic bomb on that city. On this, the forty-eighth anniversary of the bombing, Teru and Kaz paused at the main viewing area for the Peace Flame. Behind them stood a gray saddle-shaped cement structure where people often place flowers and other offerings. About twenty yards away, resting on a stand in the middle of a pond, was the Hiroshima Peace Flame. This is the home of the flame that Teru had carried for two years on her journey. Japan has promised to keep the flame lit until the world is rid of all nuclear weapons.

This was the day of the Hiroshima Peace Memorial Ceremony. Thousands of people filled Peace Park, participating in an array of activities: folding paper peace cranes, touring the museum that contains pictures and video interviews, floating small boats with candles in a pond, and viewing a partially destroyed building known as the A-Bomb Dome, which has remained untouched since the

bombing and stands as a symbol of the bomb's impact. Other people rang a "peace bell" and visited the Children's Peace Monument, dedicated to the children lost in the bombing.

Teru had spent three and a half months walking in Japan. On arriving, she was happy to be in a modern country again, after about ten months in India, Pakistan, Nepal, Thailand, Cambodia, and Vietnam. She enjoyed not having to worry about land mines on the side of the road, diseases such as malaria and dysentery, and where to get clean drinking water. She was also fortunate, yet again, to have the Nipponzan Myohoji group to house her when she arrived in Japan.

In Japan, she felt at home with the food and the mannerisms, which were similar to the ones she had grown up with, but it was also awkward at times, since she did not speak the language. Looking at her, the child of two Japanese parents, people assumed that she did, and, while Teru could understand a little Japanese, she had never learned to speak it. In fact, in many ways Japan taught her just how American she had become. This was evident in the first few weeks of the group's walk with the Nipponzan Myohoji monks and nuns. For the previous three years, the Global Walkers had adopted a very "American" system, with few schedules. Each person walked at his or her own pace, and members often talked with one another as they walked. People were free to follow their whims, to join kids at a swimming hole for several hours or to have tea at a local's home if they so desired. Everyone did as they pleased, and when people went on side trips they were trusted to catch up with the main group later.

For the Japanese monks, on the other hand, everything was scheduled. Instead of going at one's own pace, members walked in two lines, and were encouraged to beat a drum and chant along the way; talking was forbidden while peace-walking. The schedule was set at the beginning of the day and everyone was expected to follow it. This was very much an expression of the Japanese culture, which emphasizes order and the needs of the group. This structure had worked for decades on the monks' annual trek from Hiroshima to Tokyo. Now, however, they were joined by seven free-living, individualistic foreigners, many of whom

had spent the past three years practicing their own style of walking and were unaccustomed to adjusting or being told what to do. While the Japanese had a rigid hierarchy, with one senior monk in control, we were not used to such a system, and weren't eager to adopt it.

The result, as was mentioned earlier, was a split in the two groups after about two weeks. Though it may seem odd that the two groups would go separate ways because they had divergent methods of peace-walking, in the end the cultural differences were too difficult to overcome. Some of the Global Walkers – Essrea, Taz, and I – continued to walk to Hiroshima on our own, without the monks, while Teru and the others decided to join a walk for indigenous people on the northernmost Japanese island, Hokkaido. The plan was for the group heading to Hiroshima to keep the Walk going as planned, and then the groups would converge for the final few weeks, ending up in Hiroshima together. This worked out as planned. We arrived in Hiroshima, for better or worse, doing things our own way.

On August 6th, though she had just finished her journey and had good reason to celebrate her arrival in Hiroshima, Teru was pensive, awash in emotions. She did not wear her usual smile as she attempted to manage the flood of feelings running through her. This was, in part, a result of seeing the Peace Flame, her trusted companion for the first two and a half years of the journey. The sight of it reminded her how much she had missed it in the last phase of her journey, of the hundreds of nights she had slept next to it, and of all the people to whom she had showed it.

This was also the end of her journey. Life would look different from now on, though just how she did not know. She had planned for more than three years to end the Walk in Hiroshima, and, now that the day was here, she felt disoriented. She had never thought much about this final day, choosing instead to focus on taking one day at a time.

And it was a day to commemorate those who had died or whose lives had been forever changed by the nuclear bomb, called Little Boy, which had been dropped on Hiroshima on August 6, 1945, killing at least 140,000 people, mainly civilians. For Teru, this was a day not to celebrate but to grieve. As she toured the museum and viewed the other reminders of the devastation, she grieved for the people of Hiroshima who had lost friends and relatives, for the Americans who had been killed in the war, and for this world where so many people have felt the pain of war. Teru was solemn as she thought of the impact of war and nuclear weapons. This day was not about her journey; it was about remembering those who had lost their lives, and about rededicating oneself to the path of peace.

With all this occupying her attention, Teru could not appreciate what it had taken to complete her journey, the thousands of footsteps she had taken, the hundreds of people who had fed and housed her and the others, the thousands of people with whom she had interacted, and the numerous countries and cultures she traversed. It would take time for Teru to fully appreciate all that she had done, but over time she did.

The Final Years

When Teru was a young child, her mother visited a psychic to inquire about Teru's future. The psychic predicted that Teru would someday be a teacher. When Teru learned this later in life, she thought, "Teacher. I don't want to be a teacher." Though she did teach dental-hygiene classes before the Walk, she never identified herself that way. Then, several years after the Walk, while sitting in Ess's house in Boulder, Colorado, Teru said, "I always thought of a teacher as someone who gives advice and tells people what to do, and I did not want to be that. But now I see that I am a teacher as the psychic predicted. I am a teacher who teaches by example, and who reminds people of their goodness. I never knew when I was young that I could also be a teacher this way. That is the kind of teacher I want to be."

Teru's teaching was, first and foremost, about the essential goodness that exists in every person. It was when she realized this on her journey that she no longer felt alone in the world. This was one of her greatest lessons. The night before Teru flew to London to begin the European segment of the Walk, after her family and friends had held a dinner for her and given her words of encouragement, she woke from a frightful dream. In it, she was in a foreign land surrounded by hundreds of strangers. She felt completely isolated. She was not afraid for her safety, but she was, in her words, "lonely scared." She just felt alone. The dream, she surmised, revealed her greatest fear: of feeling separate, even when surrounded by people. In time, she would understand that she never really could be separate; she could only believe herself to be.

Teru emphasized this in slide shows that she gave after the Walk ended. To help her during her presentation, she had written on small note cards the main points she wanted to get across. The notes for the last slide in the presentation are below. This is what she wanted to leave people with. It seems a perfect way to end this book, for this is, in her own words, the lesson that she most wanted to convey.

Teru's final words from her post-walk talks:

"I learned from the Walk that peace lives in the hearts of all people. The greatest gift of the Walk was that it reinforced my belief that people are intrinsically, inherently, basically good. We have all the necessary tools to change, to turn around all the hatred, greed, violence, racism, and environmental degradation, and to live simply—in peace and harmony. There is much hope. We, the common people, have the power, the real power. We just need to reclaim that power.

"I haven't related anything new to you. Likely, you have heard or read all this before, maybe in different words, but the meanings are universal. My hope is to touch that place inside that reminds you of your own power and strength. Always remember, common people are capable of the most uncommon acts."

Other Walkers Speak of the Impact of Teru and the Global Walk

To end this book, I asked some of the core walkers who spent a great deal of time with Teru to share what they learned from her and from their time on the Global Walk.

Lessons from the Global Walk

By Abigail Bokaer

After finishing the walk, in 1993, I returned to my home town, Ithaca, New York, with Hilby, a man whom I'd met while walking in Pakistan. I got very busy right away, because our son Aviv was born nine months after the Walk ended and I was completing my college degree. I've been working as an elementary-school teacher since 1997. Hilby and I have a second child, a daughter named Tivona. I've been a single mom for a while now and at times when I'm caught up in "the grind" it occurs to me how very different this lifestyle is from the one I lived during the three and a half years I spent on the Global Walk.

There's very little in this "normal life" that I'm living now that compares to being outside all day long walking, watching the tiny microcosmic world inch by at the side of the road and experiencing the incredible sense of connectedness to the earth that comes with this lifestyle. I found walking for hours on end, day after day, to be meditative and healing.

The Walk was enormously transformative on a personal level for me. I joined as a child at the age of twenty and left as an adult at the age of twenty-four. Walking with others was a vital part of the experience. There was a strong sense of connectedness, not only to the land and the communities that we were walking through but also to this small group of people who walked and lived together day in and day out. A huge sense of belonging and purpose in the world came from this group. We were our own little entity, a small tribe of people, sometimes loving each other, sometimes being thoroughly sick of each other, but always with the common goal of getting up and getting down the road each day.

The group's energy was in constant flux depending on where we were, who was in the group at the time, and the external conditions that we were walking in. Teru had the amazing ability to constantly remain positive about the Walk and focused on the Walk's mission, no matter how difficult the conditions were, or how low the group's energy was. She was completely steadfast in her vision of the Walk. I remember one day, when we were walking in the middle of India on a 110-degree day, I yelled out, "Why the **** are we doing this? The Walk is a stupid waste of time!" Teru looked back at me from where she was walking, annoyed, and said, "Ab, the Walk is fine. That's just your own distress talking." At the time, I was irate, because I wanted to get her to join me in my negative banter, but she wouldn't. This was a woman who could not be swayed from her belief in what she was doing.

Teru was the core of this little group that attracted mainly people in their early twenties. We'd join her and feel strongly dedicated to the cause and the way of life of the Walk, and then eventually get fed up, or tired out, and leave. I left and rejoined the Walk several times and Teru was always there, a steady and strong force, always positive, never judging my need to take a break, but accepting with open arms when I came back to join her and the Walk. This was the kind of leader that Teru was, leading with a positive and open heart. It's no wonder that so many of us young folks were attracted to her as a guru, as a friend and a pal to walk down the road with.

My life is so different now; the twenty-two-year-old me would laugh in disbelief at the priorities, stress, and worries that weigh on my life today. The lessons that I learned from the Walk and from Teru are numerous and run deep within me. Teru's positive energy and her unyielding dedication to the Walk were a force that carried us far as a small group of people doing something both oddly off the beaten path and extraordinary.

Lessons from the Walk

By Starlit Kompost van Kriedt
(Known on the Walk as "Star")

The Walk for a Livable World showed me how a little vision can go a long way. I learned that one goal unites people's hearts and transforms everyone touched by the action. The Walk pulled itself around the world in the spirit of pilgrims with the global chorus: "We are all human; together we create culture; we are all equals in the eyes of God."

I learned that eye contact, coupled with facial expressions, can relate volumes about who we are.

I learned that travelers who slow to the pace of the locals are sincerely welcomed into the bosom of most communities.

My life now is funny. I have a school bus, a yurt, and a cedar bark tipi to live in. I caretake/own land in the Sierras with eight other strong individuals from many walks of life. We strive for community and equality, though the haze of capitalism and hierarchy sometimes blinds us to the proper/superior way to care for the land and each other.

I live with my current bun, Adam James Holmes, who is a devout fisherman, bicyclist, solar engineer, and cobb/adobe/timber framer. We have no modern refrigerator or cooking gadgets besides tubs of water and a mud stove. We have solar panels and batteries to power our lights, radio, and well pump. We grow quite a bit of our own vegetables, and have persimmon and mulberry saplings. The modern agriculture thing of growing food is new for me. For years I championed Aboriginal skills and the hunter/gatherer lifestyle.

I am a native-skills instructor and multi-cultural cosmologist. I also tan hides with egg or brain, weave strong local baskets, and harvest and store much local food. I also just got a Mennonite washing machine – it uses a hand cranker!

Judy Teru Imai has been a deep inspiration to me. She and the other Walk visionary, Joan Bokaer, had a great deal of experience with co-counseling. Teru, particularly in Europe, supported me with this process many times, particularly when my boyfriend at the time, Taz, and I broke up. When I was feeling great hurt, Teru took me aside to a cow pasture outside of a village, and encouraged me to let my feelings be expressed, to let them rip. It really helped me to get free. In the process, no one got hurt, and I felt great!

Another time she held me for hours in her golden tent, while I sobbed. The events at that time were bringing back painful memories from my past, like my brothers' deaths and my parent's divorce. I had blocked these memories out of my child-self for protection. Teru's support allowed them to surface again in a way that they could be healed. I learned that compassion is the reward for the mining of one's emotions. I owe Teru so much for her role in my life and for carrying forward the Walk (and to Joan for the original vision). The Walk vaulted my life into the stuff of mythology!

Lessons from the Global Walk

By Essrea Cherin

Teru was both a friend and teacher, as I believe she was to all of us who walked with her. One lesson that stands out in my life today is her unwavering support of each and every one of us. Her support did not come in the form of offering advice, her style was to smile, with a twinkle in her eye, and nod – regardless of what we presented to her. She would always encourage us to 'go for it' – whatever 'it' was. For Teru, the beauty was in the learning, not in making the right decision. To her, there is no right or wrong decision – it is all about the opportunity to grow and learn from one's experiences.

There were times when she was sought out for advice, but rather than proffer any, she'd find a gentle, loving and artful means to point the individual toward their heart's calling. Whatever that was, one was to follow it. If the experience brought challenges – there would be learning in that. If it brought great joy – there, too, would be lessons. Even if she personally disagreed with the choice that the advice seeker was making – she knew that we needed to come to that place of knowing on our own – not from an authority.

To this day, her example continues to guide me. When a friend comes to me in distress, I want to help him or her be free of the difficulty as quickly as possible. Often I have a deep urge to do so by telling the person what he or she should do in a situation. While there is nothing wrong or harmful in this, Teru showed me that a true teacher, a true leader, helps facilitate the person's own discovery of the answer. She knew that there was value in going through our own process and arriving at the lesson in our own way and time. So when I am faced with a situation where I am pretty sure that a friend's life will improve if, for example, he or she broke up with a difficult boyfriend or girlfriend, I remember how Teru would see it. She would know that something brought the two of them together, and instead of lecturing the person on his or her "poor choice" she would trust that through loving support and attention to the process, the person would see this in his or her own time.

The Walk has had a profound impact in other areas of my life as well. I learned and grew immeasurably from the experience. In fact, the lessons I gleaned from the Walk are so deeply woven into my very essence that I see the impact they have made on me quite regularly. There are innumerable ways that I see the walk appearing in my present. Three areas that come to mind immediately are that of spirit, simplicity and peace. When I started, I was in my mid-20's and searching for understanding with an insatiable curiosity. In the end, I transformed into a woman having lived and breathed a multitude of spiritual lessons. I got it, I got it all. Going forward I would always feel guided by spirit and a new way to understand our physical reality and the artificial constructs of our minds.

I have also found a deep appreciation for simplicity – having arrived at 'ultimate trust' allowed me to let go of more & more – no longer needing to hold tight to "stuff" and "things." Indeed, one is freer and happier with less than with more. I saw that time and again in communities through which we walked – those with less had, in fact, more – they were more relaxed, more flexible, more generous, more kind, more happy, had more sense of community, more play &

MUCH more! Having gained this insight has made such an impact on my choices since the Walk – knowing that happiness does not flow from material wealth but in following one's heart – wherever that may lead.

The third area is that I feel I finally discovered the answer to, "How can there be peace on earth?" This is something that often feels completely unattainable and out of reach. I realized in my experience on the Walk that in fact, peace ALREADY exists on Earth – just as war does. Peace is here, it is with us – it is within each and every one of us and we have an opportunity to make it with every interaction we have, every choice we make, and every thought we entertain. It is not something for the future, it is here with us now.

Having learned to follow my heart led me to my current employment situation where my experience on the Walk allows me to be somewhat of a "resident expert." We are working to create a permanent route of pilgrimage to follow in Abraham's footsteps (www.abrahampath.org) and of those on our globally dispersed team, I have years more experience as a pilgrim (especially on a non-established route). I adore offering my wisdom and knowledge on such matters as walking, faith and packing. When I first applied for my current job with the author and global peacemaker, William Ury, it was the first time since the Walk that the 4 years between 1990- 1993 were not considered an unusual omission on my resume, but a highlight dancing off the page.